Sawah cultivation in ancient Java

Aspects of development during the Indo-Javanese period, 5th to 15th century

N.C. van Setten van der Meer

Oriental Monograph Series no.22

Faculty of Asian Studies in association with
Australian National University Press, Canberra 1979

First published in Australia 1979
Second printing 1979
Third printing 1986
Set up and printed at The Australian National
University

©N.C. van Setten van der Meer 1979

This book is copyright. Apart from any fair dealing
for the purpose of private study, research, criticism,
or review, as permitted under the Copyright Act, no
part may be reproduced by any process without
written permission. Inquiries should be made to the
publisher.

National Library of Australia
Cataloguing-in-Publication entry

Van Setten van der Meer, Nancy Clare, 1918-
    Sawah cultivation in ancient Java

    (Oriental monograph series; no.22).
    Index
    Bibliography
    ISBN 0 7081 0767 2
    1. Rice - Java - History - ca.400 - ca. 1500.
    I. Title. (Series: Australian National
    University, Canberra. Faculty of Asian
    Studies, Oriental monograph series; no 22).

633.18'87'095982

Library of Congress No. 78-74667

Cover design by ANU Graphic Design
Distributed by:

        Bibliotech,
        Australian National University,
        P.O. Box 4,
        Canberra 2600
        Australia

ACKNOWLEDGEMENTS

This work was based on a thesis I submitted to the Australian National University in December 1974 for the Degree of Master of Arts (Asian Studies). My gratitude is extended to Dr Ann Kumar of the Department of Asian Civilizations for her supervision and guidance, and to Dr Soewito Santoso of the Department of Indonesian Languages and Literatures for his kind assistance with problems of translation.

To Dr J.G. de Casparis I express my sincere thanks and appreciation for his valuable comments and suggestions. To Dr Supomo also I extend my thanks for his kind help and advice.

I am indebted to Professor Samsuri, Rector of the Institute of Teacher Training in Malang and Drs Moeh Habib Mustopo, also to Mr J.W. Sulandra, Head of the East Java Division of the Department of Education and Culture, for making possible a visit to the Kali Pikatan region and an inspection of the inscriptions in the Mojokerto Museum during a visit to Indonesia in 1973.

Acknowledgement of my indebtedness would not be complete without honouring the memory of Dr R.M. Sutjipto Wirjosuparto whose help and encouragement led me to this study, and whose inspiration lives on.

CONTENTS

Acknowledgements		iii
Introduction		vii
CHAPTER ONE	SAWAH CULTIVATION IN ANCIENT JAVA	1
	The antiquity of *sawah* cultivation	
	Hazards of *sawah* cultivation	9
	Principles of irrigation used in ancient Java	21
	The Balinese *sekaha subak*	41
TWO	SAWAH CULTIVATION AT VILLAGE LEVEL	53
	Village organization	56
	Village bureaucracy	60
	Land and water rights	66
THREE	SAWAH CULTIVATION UNDER KRATON SUPERVISION	74
	The adoption of Indian principles of kingship	77
	The structure of the Indo-Javanese kingdom	84
	Women in Old Javanese agrarian society	91
	The bond between the *kraton* and the *wanua*	96
FOUR	RELIGIOUS ASPECTS OF AGRARIAN LIFE IN ANCIENT JAVA	99
	Rice-growing ceremonies	101
	Religious festivals of the agricultural year	112
	Land grant ceremonies	116
	The religious significance of cock-fighting	126
	Temples and bathing sanctuaries	130
Conclusions		133
Maps: Early irrigation regions in East Java		136
The Brantas River system		137
Abbreviations		138
Bibliography		139
Glossary		151
Index of Inscriptions		160
General Index		162

INTRODUCTION

In the period prior to the fifteenth century, there is evidence to indicate the development of comparatively large-scale irrigation farming under the administration of an Indianized court bureaucracy. From the end of the Indo-Javanese period, however, up to the introduction of modern technological methods and hydraulic installations in the colonial period, the state of *sawah*, wet-rice cultivation, is unknown. The Balinese appear to have continued to manage their *sawah* farming at the comparatively high level of organization and achievement they had reached, presumably by the fifteenth century at least, and which it appears the Javanese rice farmers had also achieved but for some reason had lost. Some scholars have considered the possibility that the Netherlands East Indies Company's forced deliveries system of the eighteenth century and the Government's Culture System of the early nineteenth century may have had some adverse effect on the efficiency of *sawah* management in Java in comparison with that in Bali. Van Vollenhoven also considers that the Government's increasing participation in agrarian matters, such as the fixing of land measurements and taxes and the re-surveying of farmlands, may have caused some disruption to age-old indigenous methods of *sawah* management.[1]

Apart from the fact that there was no active part taken by the Netherlands Government in agrarian matters in Bali, even after direct

---

1   C. van Vollenhoven. *Het adatrecht van Nederlandsch-Indië*, I, 1931, 546.

government was introduced after 1880, the Balinese *sawah* farmers' success appears to stem mainly from their efficient independently-organized irrigation associations known as *sekaha subaks*. These guild-like co-operations of *sawah* farmers who share the same water supply have existed for many centuries in Bali, but nowhere else in Indonesia's wet-rice areas does there appear to be a similar organization, although one operates in Northern Luzon and another in Madagascar. Writers of the previous century and early years of the present one were surprised to find no traces of an indigenous system of irrigation management in Java to compare with the Balinese *subaks*, but nevertheless considered it likely that a type of *subak* system had once existed in Java.

Van Eck and Liefrinck[2] considered the possibility of a Javanese origin for the Balinese *subak* associations in the kingdom of Majapahit, arguing from their assumption that Balinese law-books came from Majapahit and on the fact that the Balinese collections of *adat* and *subak* regulations were in Old Javanese. However, this theory must now be revised, since there is evidence for the existence of *subak* associations in Bali as early as the eleventh century A.D., during the reign of Airlangga's parents. There is yet earlier evidence of advanced hydraulic management in a ninth-century inscription which refers to tunnel-building.

Included in the collection of Balinese *adat* (customary law) are *kerta sima desa* and *kerta sima subak*, i.e. village laws and *subak* regulations. As part of sacred archives, usually kept in

---

[2] R. van Eck and F.A. Liefrinck, 'Kerta-sima of Gemeente-en Waterschappen-wetten op Bali', *TBG*, XXIII, 1876, 161-5.

the *kraton*, these *kerta simas* were preserved in the community concerned, although in 1876 five from major agrarian centres were found, which were translated and published. If similar collections of rules and regulations exist in private collections in Java, they have not been discovered. Since the same factors necessitating constant recopying operate in Java as in Bali, one may perhaps assume that it is unlikely that much has been preserved which would throw light on rural organization in ancient Java. The Balinese *kerta sima subaks* were written on *lontar* leaves and therefore did not last for any length of time before becoming illegible or disintegrated, due to the ravages of insects and the humidity. They have therefore been copied by countless generations of scribes but, unfortunately, only the date of re-writing the charter is recorded in this process, not the date of the original issue. Thus, the actual age of *subak* laws and regulations is unknown. Most of them, in Liefrinck's opinion, originated in remote times but additions and amendments were made by subsequent rulers. As these regulations concerning irrigation farming may indeed date from a remote period they help to throw light on the type of irrigation management which must have existed in ancient Java.

Indonesian land and water rights are very complex, even in comparatively modern times; in earlier periods the picture is not made any clearer by the lack of source material. There are only the epigraphical records and the *Nāgarakĕrtāgama* in which to search for any reference which may throw some light on agrarian administration during the Indo-Javanese period. The *Nāgarakĕrtāgama* contains information concerning rural life in the fourteenth century in East Java which can be applied to a certain extent to the period prior to the fourteenth century; this information, as well as that contained in the Balinese *kerta sima subaks* has been drawn upon in the present work, supplimented by writings and reports on laws and customs applying to the present time but which may have persisted from ancient times.

Apart from van Vollenhoven's extensive work on the subject of *adat*, which covers all facets of Indonesian customary law including rights of inheritance and the right of possession and disposal of land,[3] there is the useful volume by ter Haar, the only source concerning *adat* to appear in English translation to date.[4] The reports and writings of Dutch colonial servants and others who worked in Indonesia are to be found in various journals published in the Netherlands. Some statements by colonial officials appear to be contradictory, possibly because the writers reported on conditions as they appeared to them, which may not always have been a complete or objective view, or a correct interpretation of the evidence. Certain misunderstandings are reflected in some of these sources and they should therefore be used with caution. These works have been consulted for their wealth of information on Javanese and Balinese *adat* and methods of agricultural and village administration of recent times, which provides a background for the elucidation of material gleaned from Old Javanese and Balinese inscriptions. The present work is an investigation into various aspects of *sawah* cultivation in ancient Java using inscriptions issued during that period, with the intention of seeking evidence, however provisional at this stage of present-day knowledge of epigraphical material, of the nature and extent of irrigation systems in this period.

---

[3] C. van Vollenhoven, *Het adatrecht van Nederlansch Indië*, 1931.

[4] B. ter Haar, *Adat Law in Indonesia*, 1962.

Much information lies hidden within the inscriptions of the Indo-Javanese period, information which could help fill the gaps in our knowledge of social, economic and administrative life of Java and Bali during the period of Indianization. As so many of these inscriptions concern land transactions for various purposes, such as the acquisition of agricultural land for the upkeep of sanctuaries, or the granting of tax exemption to certain villages in return for specific services rendered, some insight into village administration and organization, taxation systems, the legal aspect of land tenure and so on, could be gained from them.

Unfortunately, by far the greater part of Indonesian epigraphical material has yet to be transcribed, translated and published. Until this formidable task has been accomplished the wealth of information many of these inscriptions contain will lie beyond the reach of students unable to read Sanskrit, Old Javanese or Old Balinese. Gaps in our knowledge of ancient Javanese and Balinese history and culture, and doubts concerning the correct interpretation of certain passages of old records, must remain for the time being, mainly due to a lack of epigraphists in this field. Buchari[5] remarks on the vast number of inscriptions still awaiting detailed study; he draws attention to the fact that, according to Damais' list of inscriptions of Java, Bali, Sumatra and Madura,[6] of the total of 290 listed, only eighty-one complete transcriptions and translations with commentaries have been published, 134 have been published in transcription only, and seventy-five have not been published at all.

---

[5] See Buchari, 'Epigraphy' in Soedjatmoko (*ed.*) in *An Introduction to Indonesian Historiography*, 1965, 48-73, concerning Indonesian epigraphy.

[6] L.C. Damais, 'Études d'epigraphie Indonesienne: III Liste des principales inscriptions datées de l'Indonésie', *BEFEO*, XLVI, 1952-4, 1-105.

Although still useful as a basis for further study of Old Javanese epigraphical material, the 125 collected transcriptions of Old Javanese inscriptions by Brandes,[7] and the thirty transcriptions by Cohen Stuart[8] contain errors and omissions. Neither volume contains translations, nor do they provide commentaries, index or glossary. They have now been replaced to a great extent by two volumes published recently by Sarkar,[9] containing 112 transcriptions and eighty-seven translations, with notes and glossaries, of Old Javanese inscriptions dating from around the fifth century to the early tenth century A.D. Besides Sarkar's work there are the two volumes by de Casparis,[10] containing transcriptions and translations, with very detailed notes and commentaries, of eighteen inscriptions from Central Java, and Stutterheim's valuable contribution to this field of study.[11] Old Balinese epigraphy has been studied by Goris[12] and van Stein Callenfels.[13] Transcriptions, in some cases with translations, of

---

[7] N.J. Krom (*ed.*), 'Oud-Javaansche oorkonden: Nagelaten transcripties van wijlen Dr. J.L.A. Brandes', *VBG*, LX, 1913.

[8] A.B. Cohen Stuart, *Kawi Oorkonden in Facsimile, met Inleiding en Transcriptie*, 1875.

[9] H.B. Sarkar, *Corpus of the Inscriptions of Java*, I and II, 1972. See also a review of these works by P.J. Zoetmulder in *BKI*, 132, 1976, 188.

[10] J.G. de Casparis, *Inscripties uit de Çailendra-tijd*, 1950, and *Selected Inscriptions from the 7th to the 9th Century A.D.*, 1956.

[11] Stutterheim's works include, besides his *Inscripties van Nederlandsche-Indie*, I, 1940, a large number of translations of Old Javanese inscriptions with notes and commentaries. For further information concerning Stutterheim's work see J.G. de Casparis, 'Historical Writing on Indonesia (Early Period), in D.G.E. Hall (*ed.*), *Historians of South East Asia*, 19, 138-41.

[12] Roelof Goris, *Prasasti Bali*, I and II, 1954.

[13] P.V. van Stein Callenfels, 'Epigraphica Balica', *VBG*, LXVI, 3, 1926.

single Old Javanese inscriptions have been published by Krom, van Naerssen, Bosch, Poerbatjaraka and others, but these are scattered through Dutch academic journals.[14] Some Old Javanese charters are included in Pigeaud's work[15] concerning the *Nāgarakĕrtāgama*, and in van Naerssen's doctoral thesis.[16] Although all these works are of great value they represent a comparatively small percentage of the total and even concerning these Buchari warns that:

> ... with the advancement of our knowledge of old languages, existing translations and transcriptions will have to be continually revised. Correspondingly, all conclusions derived from these translations will have to be re-examined.[17]

In an endeavour to interpret ancient inscriptions a conscious effort must be made to bridge the gap between modern man and the *anak thāni*, the farmers who faced the trials of pioneer rice cultivation and their descendants who continued to till the soil of their forefathers. It is through inscriptions, engraven records of the ruler's spoken word, that glimpses can be seen of another level of society, the rural community of ancient Java.

Royal edicts were mostly engraved on stone, generally in oblong form with a shaped base and top, which was sometimes crowned with a lotus. Several early inscriptions were incised on rock and some on statues. More detailed inscriptions were engraved on both front and back, and sometimes the sides, of larger upright stones and on

---

[14] Appearing mainly in *TBG* and *BKI*. Details of each inscription known at the time of publication are given in Damais' 'Liste', together with author and whereabouts of transcriptions and translations, if any.

[15] Th. G. Pigeaud, *Java in the 14th Century*, I-V, 1960-63.

[16] F.H. van Naerssen, *Oudjavaansche Oorkonden in Duitsche en Deensche Verzamelingen*, 1941, and other works.

[17] Buchari, 'Epigraphy', 50.

copper-plates. These stone and copper-plate charters, tangible evidence of the royal spoken word, were revered as sacred objects. Copper-plate inscriptions were kept within families to whom they concerned for generations, as heirlooms of great value.

The earliest Javanese inscriptions, written in Pallava script and Sanskrit language, are undated but considered to belong to the fifth century A.D. The Canggal inscription of 732 A.D., issued by the Central Javanese ruler Sañjaya, is the earliest dated inscription. The earliest known example of the Old Javanese, or Kawi script appears on the Plumpungan stone of 752 A.D. followed by the Dinaya inscription of 760 A.D. issuing from Kañjuruhan, the earliest known kingdom in East Java, although the language used in both is still Sanskrit. Also from East Java comes the earliest inscription using both Old Javanese script and Old Javanese language, the Hariñjing A charter of 804 A.D., which is also the oldest recording of an irrigation project in Java.[18]

The last stone edict written in Kawi was issued in 1486 A.D., at the close of the Indo-Javanese period. During the millenium in which Old Javanese epigraphy flourished, from the fifth to the fifteenth century, four dual language inscriptions were issued, two major charters and two shorter ones.[19] Attention is drawn to these charters for the fact that the first part of each, the part which refers to the ruler and the deities, is written in Sanskrit whereas the second part, concerning rural matters, is expressed in Old Javanese;

---

[18] See J.G. de Casparis, *Indonesian Palaeography. A History of Writings from the Beginnings to C. A.D. 1500*, 1975. This valuable work is the first to appear since Holle's volume of 'Tables' published a century ago. (K.F. Holle, *Tabel van Oud-en Nieuw-Indische Alphabetten*, 1882).

[19] Karangtěngah inscription of 824 A.D.; Siwagĕrha stone of 856 A.D.; Pereng stone of 862 A.D.; 'Calcutta Stone' of 1041 A.D.

both the Sanskrit and the Old Javanese parts, concerning the court and the village respectively, use purely Indonesian personal names and place-names.

The language used in Old Javanese and Old Balinese inscriptions is terse to the point of understatement. Sarkar remarks that the engravers of Old Javanese charters did not 'indulge in flamboyant and exaggerated eulogy of many ancient Indian inscriptions. Here the problem is not one of exaggeration but of excessive abbreviation'.[20] It is this economy of detail which gives rise to difficulties in translating the text, especially where titles, personal names and place-names may be confused. To add to the translator's problems are the many obscure Old Javanese terms found in the lengthy lists of both court and village officials. Familiarity with literary Old Javanese does not always provide an answer to the many problems of interpretation, as the language of inscriptions differs from that used in literature. Terms for agricultural measurements, land tax and rural administration do not occur in *kakawins*.

The existence of copies, made either around the time the original charter was issued or some centuries later, has contributed to the problems which beset the epigraphist, especially when endeavouring to place material in chronological order. Confusion arose in the past when scholars mistook copies for original inscriptions. Brandes was the first to discover that some inscriptions he had been studying were actually copies of older edicts.[21] The purpose of copying previously

---

[20] Sarkar, I, xii. A comparison may be made between the Hariñjing A and the Bakalan inscriptions, and the Indian Junāgarh rock inscription of Rudradaman I (unpublished translation by Professor A.L. Basham, of inscription no.67 in D.S. Sircar (ed.), *Select Inscriptions bearing on Indian history and civilization*, 1965, 175-82).

[21] Brandes realized that an inscription of 840 A.D., which he included in his edition of the *Pararaton* was a copy. See N.J. Krom, *Hindoe-Javanese geschiedenis*, 1931, 4.

issued inscriptions may have been to fulfil a desire for continuity and permanence or to establish a definite link with former dynasties in order to provide a usurper with a 'legitimate' genealogy. A notable number of copies of earlier edicts were made during the Majapahit period which may reflect a certain instability and unease within the kingdom. There are examples of copies of edicts, made by later rulers or high court dignitaries, to lend weight to their claim over land, or to proclaim the ruler's benevolence. In respect to Balinese copies Goris found that generally the copy of an original inscription was followed by a second edict or additional information, with the word *punah* or *muwah*, (in addition to) added.[22] Sarkar remarks on cases where some copper-plate inscriptions had been copied onto stone with *tinulad* (copied) added below, but this was more an exception than the rule, leading to errors in dating.[23]

Old Javanese inscriptions, with few exceptions, adhered to a certain formula during the centuries in which they were issued. Generally, they began with a record of the precise year and day of issue, followed by the full title of the ruler or high dignitary issuing the decree. The royal order was then transmitted to high-ranking officials through whose hands it would pass down to the person, religious body or secular guild in whose favour the grant was to be made. The reason, *sambhanda*, for issuing the decree was given, followed by usually detailed provisions for exempting the freehold from taxes, and for their protection from trespassers. The often extensive list of persons forbidden to trespass on the freehold land provides us with many terms for ranks and occupations within the

---

[22] Roelof Goris, *Ancient History of Bali*, 1965, 39.

[23] Sarkar, I, xii.

ancient rural administration. Long lists of various officials forbidden to enter the freehold estates are found in inscriptions as early as the Kuṭi charter of 840 A.D. and continue to the end of the Indo-Javanese period, but unfortunately the meaning of many of these words remains obscure.

The foundation ceremony, confirming a royal grant, is recorded in detail in many inscriptions and throws some light on the indigenous religious beliefs as distinct from the adopted elements of Indian ritual and attributes of Hindu deities. Participants in ceremonial proceedings, including both court and rural secular and religious officials, are listed. Their titles of rank are, with very few exceptions, purely Old Javanese. Traditional ceremonial gifts of special cloth presumably for ceremonial wear, and measures of gold or silver presented to the various officials taking part are carefully enumerated. The commemoration ritual, performed to sanctify the inscription stone or copper-plate in order to endow it with mystical power, is described in some detail in the more elaborate inscriptions.

Ninety percent of Old Javanese inscriptions concern the investiture of land grants, made for the purpose of erecting sanctuaries or funerary temples thereon, and the granting of *sawah* fields assigned for the upkeep of the freehold domain concerned. Only a few inscriptions refer specifically to irrigation projects such as dam construction or the excavation of canals to carry irrigation water.[24] With the exception of the fifth-century Tugu inscription which records the diversion of a river, the only records of hydraulic

---

[24] J.Ph. Vogel, 'The Earliest Sanskrit Inscriptions of Java', *POD*, 1925.

installations have issued from East Java.[25] Early charters from Central Java, however, refer to *sawah* cultivation and reflect a well-established centre of irrigation farming. A number of inscriptions belonging to the second half of the Indo-Javanese period contain regulations for water distribution and the dues to be paid for the use of irrigation water supplies. A few inscriptions are *jayapattras*, legal documents recording for all time the judgement of a dispute, usually over agricultural land, and the names of the party in whose favour the case was settled. There are very few *jayapattras* inscribed on stone or copper-plate; they were probably committed to *lontar* leaves only.

The majority of land grants were made in favour of religious bodies although freehold land was also assigned to individual loyal subjects and to certain guilds by a ruler who desired to reward faithful service. Generally the establishing of a freehold, a *sīma*, was the ruler's prerogative but there are recorded instances of land grants having been made by high court dignitaries, who apparently possessed sufficient authority to dispose of land to favoured persons.

Inscriptions recording land grants usually contain exact details of the 'marking out', or surveying, of the land, in which the boundaries are designated either by landmarks such as hills, rivers or mountains, or by lineal measurements together with a record of place-names of the bordering village territory. Names of the representatives or 'witnesses' to the actual measuring of the fields,

---

[25] The Harinjiñg inscription (P.V. van Stein Callenfels, 'De inscriptie van Sukabumi', *MKAW-L*, LXXVIII, 1934, 116-17) the Bakalan inscription (Kromodjojo Adi Negoro, *Oud-Javaansche Oorkonden*, 1923) the Kĕlagyan inscription (Kromojojo Adi Negoro, *Oud-Javaansche Oorkonden III*, 1923, and Sutjipto Wirjosuparto, *Apa sebabnya Kediri dan sekitarnya tampil kemuka dalam sedjarah*, 1958, 75-9) the Kandangan inscription (P.V. van Stein Callenfels, 'De inscriptie van Kandangan', *TBG*, LVIII, 1919, 339).

elders of the surrounding villages who were present at the ceremony to verify the legality of the land transaction, are recorded; also the place where the engraved stone recording these details was erected and consecrated, or the copper-plate deposited, as the case may have been. The act of consecrating the stone or copper-plate recording the *sīma*, gift of land, and the details of the transfer, made the deed legal and binding for all time and was a valid 'document' for the recipient family for generations to come. Because a magico-religious relationship has always existed between the Indonesian people and the land on which they lived, worked and died, the changing status or ownership of any land was regarded as highly significant by all inhabitants of the immediate neighbourhood.[26]

The information contained in many Old Javanese inscriptions concerning newly-established *sawah* lands, such as border delineations and instructions on the distribution and payment of irrigation water, may give some idea of when the districts concerned were opened up. For example, the Trailokyapuri charters of 1486 A.D.[27] give detailed border limits from which it can be seen how the population of East Java must have increased and the number of villages multiplied. Nearly all the listed villages supplying witnesses to the establishing of a freehold domain were in the immediate neighbourhood, according to Maclaine Pont over a distance of only thirteen kilometres. Five and a half centuries earlier, during Sindok's reign, an entire district had been scarcely

---

[26] Mallinckrodt refers to the close attachment the farmers felt for their land. (J. Mallinkrodt, 'Grond en Waterrecht in de afdeeling Boetoek', *Het Koloniaal Tijdscrift*, No.1, 15 January 1924, 66. See also Peter Suzuki, *The Religious System and Culture of Nias*.

[27] OJO XCIV-V.

sufficient to provide the number of witnesses required to attend the consecration ceremony connected with a land transfer.[28]

In this work attention has been directed to *sawah* farming in East Java in ancient times, and to the Kali Pikatan region in particular. The development of East Java during the early part of the Indo-Javanese period appears to have been neglected by scholars of the past, commencing with Brandes who considered the region to be little more than a wilderness at this time. However, a study of the inscriptions has shown that in East Java an established kingdom, apparently based on *sawah* cultivation, existed as early as agrarian kingdoms in Central Java. As already noted it is from East Java that the earliest epigraphical reference to irrigation management comes, providing not only evidence of hydraulic organization on a comparatively advanced scale, but the earliest example of privately-owned irrigation works, in the Hariñjing project of the Bhagawanta Bāri.

As this work includes material which applies to the present as well as to ancient Java difficulties arise in the use of a spelling system. Many geographical names, and some anthropological terms used herein are still current today. Therefore, to conform to present day usage, where these occur in the present day context the Indonesian orthography is used, except in quotations. Where the work concerns material drawn from Old Javanese sources, or concerns the Indo-Javanese period an appropriate spelling system is used.

---

[28] H. Maclaine Pont, 'Eenige Oudheidkundige Gegevens Omtrent de Middeleeuwschen bevloeingstoestand van de zoo-genaamde "woeste gronden van de Lieden van Trik" ', *OV*, 1926, 103. See also P.V. van Stein Callenfels, 'Bijdrage tot de Topographie van Oost Java in de Middeleeuwen, II', *OV*, Bijlage E, 82f.

CHAPTER ONE

SAWAH CULTIVATION IN ANCIENT JAVA

THE ANTIQUITY OF SAWAH CULTIVATION IN JAVA

Wet-rice cultivation in Southeast Asia is of acknowledged antiquity but its place of origin, whether, for instance, it may have been in Yunnan[1] or in Northwest Thailand,[2] is a subject of debate among scholars at the present time. There are also diverging opinions concerning the question of when wet-rice farming was introduced to island Southeast Asia, or even whether it evolved as a matter of course independently in certain regions within the island world and subsequently spread further eastwards. Spencer, for example, considers that wet-rice cultivation was transmitted at a very early date to the islands of Southeast Asia, for example Northern Luzon, Western Sumatra, Java and the southern part of Celebes (Sulawesi) as well as offshoots to Ceylon (Sri Lanka) and Madagascar.[3]

Fisher states that in Southeast Asia during the Neolithic period there already existed a culture not inferior to that of India - a culture with a matrilinear social structure, pile houses, highly developed seamanship - and irrigated rice cultivation.[4] Lekkerkerker, although he concedes that dry-rice cultivation was probably brought

---

[1] Chang Chih Kwang, *The Archaeology of Ancient China*, 1968, 148.

[2] Solheim, Wm II, 'An Earlier Agricultural Revolution', *Scientific American*, April 1972, 34-41.

[3] See J.E. Spencer, 'The Migration of Rice from Mainland Southeast Asia into Indonesia', in Jacques Barrau (ed.), *Plants and the Migrations of Pacific Peoples*, 1963, 82-9.

[4] C.A. Fisher, 'A View of Southeast Asia', in R.L. Singh (ed.), *Rural Settlement in Monsoon Asia*, 1972, 6.

to Indonesia from the mainland at a very early point in time, considers that wet-rice cultivation was discovered independently in Java.[5] Sutjipto Wirjosuparto advances the theory that bearers of the Dong-son culture, arriving from the mainland of Southeast Asia during the centuries just prior to the Christian era, made their way slowly along the Brantas valley, probably reaching as far as Kediri, where they settled down to dry-rice farming, a practice they had brought with them from their homeland, but that year after year the periodic flooding of the Kali Brantas would have ruined much of these crops, until by trial and error, the farmers learnt to contend with the situation by building small dams and levies.[6] Perhaps thus, by the dictates of nature, the long history of *sawah* cultivation in this part of East Java began.

Groslier considers that irrigation techniques used in Indo-China were introduced from India and were India's 'most important gift to Indo-China'.[7] Certainly it is considered by many scholars that the Indians introduced more advanced forms of irrigation management; for example an Indian-type hydraulic system operated in Cambodia.[8] Schrieke remarks that the Indians probably brought certain improvements for irrigation and methods of fertilizing, and he mentions the introduction of the water-wheel and the sickle,[9] but

---

[5] See C. Lekkerkerker, *Land en Volk van Java*, 1928, 258-9.

[6] R.M. Sutjipto Wirjosuparto, *Apa sebabnya Kediri dan daerah sekitarnya tampil kemuka dalam sedjarah*, 1958, 86.

[7] B.P. Groslier, 'Our Knowledge of Khmer Civilization: a reappraisal', *The Journal of the Siam Society*, XLVIII, 1, June 1960, 1-28.

[8] Groslier, *Angkor et le Cambodge au XVIe siècle d'auprès les sources portugaises et espagnoles*, 1958, 107-12.

[9] B.J.O. Schrieke, 'Eenige opmerkingen over ontleening in de Cultuur-ontwikkeling', *Djawa*, VI, 2, 1927, 93.

Lekkerkerker points out that in Java there was no water-wheel and the irrigation system of India was never used there.[10] Fisher also maintains that although all the main rice growing areas of Southeast Asia acquired basic methods of irrigation management from India, Java was the exception.[11] Pigeaud writes that the laying out of *sawahs* and the regulation of water supplies by dams, canals and so on date from Java's 'primeval' civilization before Indian influence.[12] Archaeological evidence in the form of tool finds might give a more precise indication of the period when wet-rice cultivation began; the tools concerned are the *pacul* and the *ani-ani*. Finds of stone adzes such as the *pacul* indicates that wet-rice farming was practised at a very early period in Java. Sutjipto Wirjosuparto draws attention to the discovery of *paculs* over a wide area in Java, which, as this tool is obviously not an implement for *ladang* use, bears witness to the practice of *sawah* cultivation in Java as early as the Neolithic period.[13] Recent finds from New Guinea, as well as contemporary practice there, suggest that many farm implements may have been of wood, and therefore not likely to show up in archaeological excavations.[14]

---

[10] Lekkerkerker, 'Verbetering en vermeerdering van cultuurgrond op Java', *De Indische Gids*, LI, 1, 1929, 536.

[11] C.A. Fisher, *South-east Asia*, 1965, 75.

[12] Th. Pigeaud, *Java in the 14th Century*, IV, 1962, 494.

[13] Sutjipto Wirjosuparto, 84. Concerning Neolithic tools used for agricultural purposes see C.R. Hooijer, *Indonesian Prehistoric Tools. A Catalogue of the Houbolt Collection*, 1969.

[14] See Grith Lerche and Axel Steenberg, 'Observations on Spade-cultivation in the New Guinea Highlands', *Tools & Tillage*, II, 2, 1973, 87-104 and John Nilles, 'Digging sticks, spades, hoes, axes and adzes of the Kuman people in the Bismark Mountains in East-Central New Guinea', *Anthropos*, XXXVI-XLII, 1942-45, 205-12.

The name Yawadwipa, used by Indian writers suggests that they saw much grain growing there in the second century A.D. The Canggal inscription, written in Sanskrit in 732 A.D. records that there was 'a great island called Yawa, abundantly supplied with grain and other seeds and rich in gold-mines ....'[15] Veth considers the use of the word *yawa*, in Dyak *yawae*, in Batak *yaba ure*, (*ure* having the same meaning as Javanese *awut* grain) is proof that rice was cultivated in Java before the coming of the Indians and by the time they were visiting the island, in quantities large enough to attract their comment,[16] which might indicate the double cropping which *sawah* cultivation allows. Veth endeavours to prove his theory by linguistics and ethnology: he notes that the Filipinos from the interior, who never had contact with Indians and had no plough, were *sawah* cultivators.[17]

Wheatley, in his monograph concerning agricultural terracing, gives an interesting account of a form of irrigation used in ancient times in Indo-China which appears to have parallels with that practised in some parts of ancient Java and for that reason a passage from Wheatley's work is included. He writes:

---

[14] (contd)
The Kuman practise a 'trenching culture' or draining system on sloping ground.

[15] The Canggal inscription, line 7,
H.B. Sarkar, *Corpus of the Inscriptions of Java*, I, 1971, 18. The name Yawadwipa also occurs in Airlangga's inscription of 1037 A.D. (OJO LXI, line 20).

[16] P.J. Veth, *Java*, 1, 20.

[17] Veth. The achievements of the Filipino terrace cultivators can be studied in works such as those of H. Otley Beyer, 'The Origin and History of the Philippine Rice Terraces', *Proceedings of the Eighth Pacific Science Congress*, 1953, 387-9; Henry T. Lewis, *Ilocano Rice Farmers. A comparative study of two Philippine barrios*, 1971; F.M. Keesing, *Ethnology of Northern Luzon*, 1962, and others.

> ... there is indisputable evidence of a local terracing tradition of a very distinctive kind. It occurs in association with numerous villages on the Gio-Linh uplands in Quang-Tri province, ... It comprises discrete series of stone-embanked terraces for both farming and ritual purposes, each series being combined with one or more tanks and an irrigation system. The significant point is that each of these systems - and they are rather numerous - was designed as a complete regional scheme. Although the units involved, whether terrace, basin or flume, were of simple construction, they were combined into a complex series in such a way as to facilitate the management of an entire socio-economic unit, namely the territory and persons constituting a group of families or even a whole village. A representative system would include, at decreasing elevations, the following elements: (i) one or more dry-field terraces constructed at the highest point of the village territory; (ii) an upper tank serving as a reservoir for the collection of water from stream or spring; (iii) a lower tank to serve domestic needs of the village or family, particularly washing and bathing; (iv) and one or more fairly extensive wet-field terraces. Below the upper tank water is led from level to level by a series of flumes and channels, the whole system being the expression of a preconceived and carefully executed plan.[18]

Wheatley goes on to point out that each complex was so integrated as to suggest that 'it did not develop piecemeal'. Bridges, causeways and staircases were found, and 'cult objects such as menhirs, stone seats, earthen pyramids and circular mounds sited at various points within the system'. There are analogous systems of terracing among the Angami Nagas, in North Cahar, Nias, and in Java and Bali, Wheatley adds.[19] Wheatley has been quoted at length because it may be that similar irrigation complexes in Java await the archaeologist.

---

[18] Paul Wheatley, 'Agricultural Terracing', *Pacific Viewpoint*, VI, 2, Sept. 1965, 135-6.

[19] Wheatley, 139.

The earliest centres of *sawah* cultivation in Java developed steadily over a long period of time towards the formation of small centres of growing influence, certain of which became more powerful as time went on. These small irrigation centres did not arise with the coming of Indian influence, although they had their most glorious blooming during the middle of the Indo-Javanese era. As van Leur writes:

> The pattern of the states as they came to the fore in the Hindu-Javanese period - a central royal authority with a sacral significance and a patrimonial bureaucracy, based on a population strictly domesticated, in the villages and carrying on *sawah* farming on the plains; a political and social life determined by the harvest and a taxation system of crop tithes in kind - can only have arisen in a formative process of ages and ages and can only be viewed as the outgrowth of the Indonesian civilization of the new stone age and bronze age. It is technologically impossible for any colonization by Hindus, whether of traders or Brahmins, to have been able to accomplish anything in this field in the short period their presence there is proved by documents. The complex of governmental technique and sacral organization can only have arisen slowly on an indigenous Indonesian basis.[20]

According to Adams the growth of irrigation societies follows two stages which he considers as: 1) *the Formative to the Florescent*, from the beginnings of irrigation and sedentary farming to a rapid growth wherein the surplus is largely in the hands of a priestly hierarchy, with consequent building of monumental religious structures in urban centres and the beginnings of warfare; 2) *the*

---

[20] J.C. van Leur, *Indonesian Trade and Society* (2nd ed.), 1967, 256-7. Van Leur refers to Krom's opinion concerning Pūrṇavarman's inscription of the fifth century and the fact that it mirrors a level of civilization which could not have developed during the twenty-two years of Pūrṇavarman's reign but which must be conceived in terms of decades and centuries. (Van Leur, 255-6).

Dynastic, with a separation and institutionalizing of secular-political and religious-economic controls in true urban centres.[21] Collier divides the development of irrigation societies into four categories as: 1) *Early Formative*, a period where some form of irrigation existed; 2) *Late Formative*, a period of expanding irrigation systems; 3) *Regional Florescence*, full exploitation of the technology which was developing in the formative period, with intensive agriculture based on elaborate irrigation systems and an increasing importance of the warrior class; and 4) *Empire*, with land controlled by the state, taxation in the form of labour on state agricultural lands and on public works, as well as service in the army, personal service to the ruler and the nobility. The surpluses of the state are used to support the state religion, the government hierarchy, the army and the nobility, and for redistribution to the commoners.[22]

The earliest centres of wet-rice cultivation in Java would certainly have been on a small scale, consistent with Adams' and Collier's theory of development. The nuclear village settlements, administered by a head and a council of elders, would, over a long period of time, have developed into irrigation centres administered by a central authority. As revealed in early inscriptions these centres, with outlying rural branches managed by court officials, flourished in Central and in East Java. The early village administration would have organized the construction of small dams, made of bamboo and branches, across streams and simple embankments around natural depressions,

---

[21] Robert Adams, 'Developmental stages in Ancient Mesopotamia' in Julian H. Steward and others, *Irrigation Civilizations: a comparative study*, 1955, 6-17.

[22] Donald Collier, 'Development of civilization on the coast of Peru', in Julian H. Steward and others, *Irrigation Civilizations: a comparative study*, 1955, 19-27.

which would have served as tanks for village use. This simple hydraulic technology developed and progesssed to the large-scale irrigation complexes of dams, reservoirs, bridges and canals which must have existed at least by the time of the Śailendras of Central Java and contemporary kingdoms in East Java, and certainly by the reign of Balitung. Even if irrigation technology originally developed independently of India, Indian principles of kingship and administration undoubtedly gave impetus to the further development of larger irrigation centres, at a time when Java was ready to pass to the florescent stage of development, if we adhere to Adams' and Collier's theories. The ultimate development of irrigation organization in Java took place in East Java in the thirteenth century with the bringing under control of the forest lands of Trik, which became the great kingdom of Majapahit.

Wolters, recalling the finding of a Buddha image dating from the fifth or sixth century at Jember in East Java, says that:

> In assessing the likelihood of thriving settlements in eastern Java at least as old as the first reference to P'o-li in the fifth century, [in the Chinese annuals] one must not forget the Brantas and Bengawan Solo rivers, whose valleys probably developed a wet-rice culture in very early times .... Nothing is in fact more likely than the existence of an eastern Javanese principality in the fifth, sixth and early seventh centuries, worthy of a visit by Ch'ang Chün, and capable of sending envoys to China.[23]

The earliest recorded knowledge of systematic irrigation in East Java is found in the Hariñjing inscription of 804 A.D.,[24] recording

---

[23] O.W. Wolters, *Early Indonesian Commerce: a study of the origins of Srivijaya*, 1967, 201.

[24] Dated 784 A.D. according to P.V. van Stein Callenfels, 'De inscriptie van Sukabumi', *MKAW-L*, 1934, 116.

the building of a dam and the excavation of a conduit to connect the Kali Hariñjing to the larger Kali Konto north-east of Keḍiri. Van Stein Callenfels remarks that Brandes was incorrect when he presumed that in the Middle Ages only Central Java was developed to any extent and was familiar with Indian culture, and that East Java was little more than a wilderness,[25] when in fact at the time of the earliest reference to *sawah* farming in inscriptions of Central Java there already existed an important irrigation work in East Java. The cultural development of East Java at that time is reflected in another inscription, the Dinaya stone dating from 760 A.D.,[26] which provides evidence of a kingdom well established by the eighth century. The region to the south-east of old Majapahit, where the Pikatan, Kromong and Landean Rivers flow down from the Anjasmoro Ranges, was apparently an established rice-growing area by the beginning of the tenth century, as indicated in Mpu Siṇḍok's Sarangan charter[27] of 929 A.D. and the Bakalan inscription issued by Rakryān Mangibil.[28]

THE HAZARDS OF SAWAH CULTIVATION IN ANCIENT JAVA

The environment in which early man struggled to establish *sawah* cultivation in East Java was governed by a harsh and unrelenting nature in the shape of the great turbulent Kali Brantas and its tributaries and restless volcanic mountains, particularly the Kelud. Judging by ancient records of dam building and irrigation control, as well as the archaeological remains of some of those hydraulic works

---

[25] Van Stein Callenfels, 125.

[26] Sarkar, I, 25-9.

[27] OJO XXXVII.

[28] OJO XLIV.

still to be seen, the *sawah* farmers succeeded in overcoming great odds to gain a foothold in areas which were to become prosperous regions of *sawah* cultivation during the Indo-Javanese period.

As van Naerssen points out, the Kali Brantas and the Kelud volcano have over the centuries brought both prosperity and tragedy to East Java: prosperity in the form of rich volcanic soils suited to *sawah* cultivation, and tragedy in the form of periodic floods which create havoc in cultivated areas.[29] These giants of nature, the Brantas and the Kelud, undoubtedly played a significant role in the development of agriculture in East Java from the earliest stages of *sawah* cultivation onwards. The enormous amount of material ejected by the Kelud at every violent eruption directly affected the Kali Brantas, and still does.[30]

The *Pararaton* records nine Kelud eruptions in the space of less than 200 years, between the years 1311 and 1481 A.D. Historically, the most interesting of these eruptions occurred in 1334, an event which coincided with Hayam Wuruk's birth. Fortunately for historians the *Pararaton* record confirms an event which, had there only been the *Nāgarakĕrtāgama*'s reference to it, may have been treated as merely a literary myth. In the *Nāgarakĕrtāgama*, canto 1, stanza 4 reads:

1. In the *Shaka*-year seasons-arrows-sun (1256 = 1334 A.D.), it is said, at his birth, the Prince has been inaugurated already as *Prabhu*.

---

[29] F.H. van Naerssen, 'De Brantas en haar waterwerken in den Hindu-Javaanschen tijd', *De Ingenieur*, 7, 1938, A65.

[30] Purbo Hadiwidjojo and I. Surjo report that during the last two eruptions in 1951 and 1966, an estimated amount of 282 million centimetres of material has been produced which, they say, will affect the hydrologic equilibrium of the Kali Brantas. (M.M. Purbo Hadiwidjojo and I. Surjo, *Volcanic Activity and its Implications on Surface Drainage: the case of the Kelut volcano as an example*, July 1968, 2.)

2. as a *porphyrogenetos* Protector in Kahuripan; the tokens of His being superhuman, wonderful, were:

3. an earthquake, the earth rumbled, rain of ashes, thunder, flashes of lightning turning about in the sky,

4. the mountain Kampud[31] collapsed, annihilated were the bad people, the rascals, dead without gasp.[32]

Prapañca's account of the supernatural omens surrounding his royal master's birth, even though composed for a different reason, still gives us some indication of the magnitude of the fearful, and historical, event of the Kelud eruption. Prapañca turned the Kelud catastrophe to Hayam Wuruk's advantage by interpreting it as a supernatural event, signifying that Girinātha, Lord of the Mountain, was incarnate in the infant prince, who thus was destined to attain the throne and rid the world of evil.

The *Pararaton* identifies the 1334 A.D. eruption as *bañu piṇḍah*.[33] According to Pigeaud, *bañu piṇḍah*, moving water, is an apt description of the streams of hot water and lava that apparently flowed down from the Kelud crater lake, inundating and devastating the countryside, a phenomenon of so many Kelud eruptions in historic times. Van Hinloopen Labberton, on the other hand, maintains that *bañu piṇḍah* signified a change in the course of the Kali Brantas caused by the Kelud eruption, a change due to blockage caused by volcanic

---

[31] Identified with the Kelud volcano.

[32] Th. Pigeaud, *Java in the 14th Century*, III, 1960, 4. Maclaine Pont refers to an earthquake which apparently occurred about this time, affecting the Majapahit inland harbour of Canggu. (Maclaine Pont, 'Aantekeningen bij het artikel van Dr van Stein Callenfels: "Bijdragen tot de Topographie van Oost-Java in de Middeleeuwen"', *OV*, 1926, 91.)

[33] The *Pararaton*, 28, line 16, reference by Pigeaud, IV, 8.

material, deflecting the river westwards.[34] Archaeological evidence points to fairly dramatic changes in the Brantas course during the latter part of the Indo-Javanese period, a phenomenon discussed below.

Besides the Kali Brantas and the Kelud volcano the part played by the Arjuna volcanic group and the Kali Pikatan and her tributaries in shaping the course of economic and cultural history in East Java should not be overlooked. It is possible that the region around the Pikatan, Kromong and Landean Rivers was already an area of *sawah* cultivation as early as the oldest known irrigated regions around Kediri and Malang. Maclaine Pont, reporting on his field study of ancient irrigation systems in this part of East Java, emphasises the significance of the region south of ancient Majapahit, i.e. in the valleys of the Pikatan and the Kromong Rivers.[35] This area will be further discussed below.

The Arjuna and at least two of her five craters were apparently active in very remote times and have since become dormant or extinct. There are no records of Arjuna eruptions and one can assume that with her Widadaren and Penanggungan craters she was dormant by the temple-building period of the Indo-Javanese era, as all three peaks have temple ruins on their high slopes or summits. Previous volcanic activity in the Arjuna, on a gigantic scale, must have forced a magma passage through to the Welirang, the youngest crater northwest of the mother volcano. This outlet in the Welirang was probably active during the Indo-Javanese period, possibly with dire results to settlements along the Pikatan, Kromong and Landean Rivers. The long

---

[34] See D. van Hinloopen Labberton, 'Oud-Javaansche gegevens omtrent de vulkanologie van Java', *Djawa*, I, 3, 1921, 197.

[35] Maclaine Pont, 94 and 98.

Anjasmoro Range runs westward from the Arjuna along the southwest slopes of the Welirang, the foothills reaching to the outer region of the old Majapahit kingdom. It is down from the Welirang slopes and along the Anjasmoro foothills that the Pikatan, Kromong and Landean Rivers run their course.

The question arises, to what extent was ancient Java affected by volcanic activity. In both Central and East Java the course of history must have been greatly affected by periodic volcanic eruptions.[36] Old Javanese records,[37] and geological evidence point to the occurrence of eruptions on a gigantic scale during the Indo-Javanese period. Archaeological evidence reveals that until the eighteenth century the Borobudur, Prambanan and Sewu temples were buried under volcanic ash deposits and apparently more than once the Mendut terrain has been submerged under mud and sand-flows moving southwards from Gunung Merapi. The entire lower levels of Candi Prambanan were found to be under the present ground level at the time of excavation and some three metres of volcanic ash had to be removed from the site of Candi Mendut in order to reach the old temple forecourt.[38]

---

[36] In Java there are 112 volcanos, some active, others dormant. Since 1600 A.D. alone there have been nineteen known violent eruptions, bringing devastation to agricultural areas.

[37] The *Nāgarakĕrtāgama* and the *Pararaton*. It is possible that the inscriptions OJO LXI (Kĕlagyan) and OJO LXII (Calcutta Stone) refer to the results of volcanic action.

[38] See van Hinloopen Labberton, 192. The removal of the seat of government from Central Java to East Java in the tenth century as a result of volcanic activity need not be an untenable theory. Buchari also suggests the possibility that a Merapi eruption caused the transfer of the centre of authority to East Java. (Buchari, 'Epigraphy', 70). Frequent volcanic eruptions must have taken their toll on the economy in ancient Java, as they have in more recent times. The 1462 and 1481 Kelud eruptions may have contributed to economic weakness in a declining Majapahit.

Volcanoes: There are several kinds of volcanoes. Some erupt once then become extinct, some erupt violently over a long interval of time, such as Krakatoa,[39] causing enormous damage. Others, like the Kelud, erupt at regular and frequent intervals. A volcano is not necessarily a mountain but material ejected usually forms one: all the volcanic mountains in Java have been built up in this way, by 'explosion' layers of sand, stone and ash, and by 'effusion' layers of lava. These mountains are known as stratigraphic volcanoes. The material ejected during a volcanic eruption consists of hot gases in the form of steam, sulphur compounds and carbon dioxide, liquids in the form of water and molten rock (lava) and solids in the form of lava fragments which consolidate either before ejection or during their flight through the air. These fragments include frothy lava (pumice) and rounded masses of lava known as 'bombs', together with ash or very fine particles of molten lava which is blown into the air, to settle over the land sometimes hundreds of kilometres from the actual eruption.

Lava may vary in composition, being either acid or basic. The basic lava of the Javanese volcanoes is more fluid than the acid lava of Sumatran volcanoes which renders soil unfit for rice cultivation. Because of its mobility the lava flows quickly and spreads out evenly, depending on the amount ejected and the terrain over which it flows. These lava flows, consisting of scoriae, lapilli and ash etc., are known in Java as *ladu*. Such lava flows may have a temperature of 400 degrees Celsius on the surface, although lava may reach an interior temperature of 900 degrees Celsius. Often, large volumes of water

---

[39] Krakatoa lay dormant for 200 years, then exploded in 1883 with such violence that two-thirds of the island were blown away. Ash remained in the atmosphere for several years, causing brilliant sunsets around the world.

flow with the *ladu*, either from the rainfall or from a crater lake, forming a muddy material known as *lahar*, mud flow. There are two kinds of *lahar*, a primary or eruption flow, which originates from volcanic eruption breaking through a crater lake, and a secondary or rain *lahar*, formed by rainwater falling on the slopes of the volcano and mixing with the *ladu* material. Primary *lahars* are hot but secondary ones may be either hot or cold. Heat may be preserved within the hot *lahars* for months or even years, depending on the thickness of the deposit.[40]

Both *ladu* and *lahar* streams flow quickly in search of any depression or river bed in the vicinity of the volcano. Sometimes a lava stream will fill an upper ravine and flow on to another on its downward journey. Because of the high density of the *lahar* stream it flows with increasing speed through the lava material, becoming a hot *lahar* through mingling with the hot masses of the *ladu* as it nears the lower mountain slopes. Both primary and secondary *lahars* are treacherous, causing extensive damage as they flow, and because of their high density and high velocity and temperature they may destroy bridges, dams and other solid constructions or leave them buried as they flow on relentlessly.[41]

Ash and sand layers which settle on the volcanic cone are eventually carried downwards to become rich tuff deposits on the hill slopes and valleys. The crater wall is usually several kilometres

---

[40] Measured during the Gunung Agung eruption in 1963. The temperature of the Gunung Agung *lahars* after one year was as high as 70 degrees Celsius (Purbo Hadiwidjojo and I. Surjo, p.3.).

[41] For example, in Bali the results of the violence of the Gunung Agung eruption in recent times is still visible. Purbo Hadiwidjojo and I. Surjo, p.3, note 'that primary *lahars* have an average velocity of 6-5 metres per second', estimated during the last Kelud eruption of 1966. Velocity in the upper course of a *lahar* flow is still higher, sometimes reaching twelve metres per second.

long and the crater itself may be very deep. There is an ever present danger of the crater walls collapsing, thus releasing from the crater lake immense volumes of water to inundate the surrounding area, causing great loss of life and devastation to farming districts; as in the catasthrophe of 1875, when the Kelud crater lake burst its walls resulting in a flood which destroyed 1,579 *bahus* of *sawah*, 788 *bahus* of dry-field farmland and 1,451 homes.[42]

Rainfall: Robert Ho, writing of the effects of rainfall, remarks that intense rainfall is directly responsible for floods and erosion. For example, in Java, one milimetre of soil over the entire catchment basin can be removed per hour by heavy rainfall. Such intensities, Ho points out, pose almost insoluble problems of accommodating large quantities of run-off water and silt brought down from built-up or denuded areas.[43] As Purbo Hadiwidjojo and I. Surjo observe, 'run-off waters are the most dominant geomorphic agency' in Indonesia, where an annual rainfall of 2,000 mm. is no exception. According to these geologists, although rainfall records have been kept and discharge measurements of major rivers have been made for a century or more these records were not made for scientific purposes and therefore there is no data available concerning the distribution of rainfall over the entire area of volcanoes or the amount of annual erosion occurring. Consequently, very little is known for scientific use of the behaviour of Indonesia's rivers.[44]

---

[42] Veth, *Java*, III, 1907, 752.

[43] Robert Ho, *Environment, Man and Development*, 1962, 6, referring to J.W. van Dijk and V.K.R. Ehrecron 'The different rate of erosion between two adjacent basins in Java', *Dienst v.d. Landbouw*, LXXXIV, 1949.

[44] Purbo Hadiwidjojo and I. Surjo, 8.

Rivers: The Brantas, East Java's major river and an important waterway in ancient times, was known during the Indo-Javanese period as Bangawan – 'Lord of the Waters'.[45] This great river provided the irrigation water for the earliest *sawahs* established along her valley and plain. As *sawah* cultivation developed and spread, by cultivators moving ever further inland, the Brantas tributaries also played their part in the long history of wet-rice cultivation in East Java; it is the Brantas, however, that has dominated the fortunes and misfortunes of countless generations of rice farmers. Throughout history to the present day, the Kali Brantas has been notoriously uncontrollable. The river's course changed dramatically several times during the Indo-Javanese period, a factor we should not ignore when considering the development of *sawah* cultivation in East Java during this period. Over the centuries sand masses from the Kelud volcano have been washed down to the Brantas and, carried along by the current, have at times blocked certain points along the river course causing the powerful current to seek a new direction and carve out a new bed.[46] This

---

[45] According to van Naerssen ('De Brantas en haar waterwerken' A65), who interprets Bangawan as 'zegenrijke Heer der Wateren'. Sutjipto Wirjosuparto (*Apa sebabnya* 65-6) refers to the Brantas as Bangawan – 'sungai besar' (large river), named thus because of the significant role the river played in the history and development of the time. In the Suradakan charter of 1447 A.D. the Brantas still bore the name Bangawan, which was later transferred to the Solo River. (Muhammad Yamin, *Petulisan Widjaya-Parakrama-Wardana dari Surodakan (Kediri), dengan bertarich sjaka 1368-T.M. 1447*, Oct. 1962).

[46] The fourteenth century Trawulan inscription reveals a systematic listing of ferry places along both the Brantas and the Solo Rivers. Place-names along the Kali Solo are still to be found on the river's present course whereas many of those listed along the Brantas in the fourteenth century are now situated inland from its present course. (See P.V. van Stein Callenfels and L. van Vuuren, 'Bijdrage tot de topographie van de residencie Soerabaja in de 14th eeuw', *TAG*, XLI, Jan. 1923, 67-81.)

creates difficulties even today, despite the greatly increased technical knowledge at man's disposal. That the ancient Javanese cultivators also were forced to overcome these formidable obstacles, threatening possible flood and famine, is certain.

The most dangerous flood points along the Brantas are at Karangrejo and Kertosono in the Kediri region and at Serbo in the Surabaya area. The bends in the river course at these points collect an enormous amount of volcanic material, especially during the first few years after an eruption. Between Kediri and Kertosono the river level is higher than the surrounding land and therefore must be diked. This is a notorious flood area at the present day and probably also at an earlier period. At Kemiri the first branching of the river's course northwards occurs: the same northerly direction occurs again at Gedek, after which the river is forced back to the foothills again at Mojokerto, continuing along the foothills to Serbo. At this point a spur of hills causes the river to curve southwards sharply and it is here that a break occurred in 1037 A.D.[47] causing much loss of farmlands and economic disruption.

The break in the river bank was obviously caused by a blockage at the sharp bend of the river course at Serbo, and must have occurred at the point where the Kali Mas now bends by the bridge at Waringin Anom, a little north of Waringin Pitu (old Waringin Sapta). The break caused the river to stream westwards, in the general direction of the present course of the Kali Porong. After the ruler, Airlangga, repaired the break by constructing dams at Waringin Sapta and at

---

[47] Recorded in the Kĕlagyan inscription, OJO LXI, issued by King Airlangga. (See map 2, p.137).

Kelagen, the river once again flowed to the north.[48] The Kali Brantas which flowed past Waringin Sapta in the eleventh century A.D. now flows some two kilometres to the north of the old course.

Two hundred and fifty years after the river break in 1037 A.D. the Brantas again changed its course. According to the *Pararaton*, the town of Pamotan was situated north of the river in 1294 A.D.; thus the point where the two Brantas arms, the Kali Mas and the Kali Porong, branch away from each other was at Serbo and not at Mojokerto as at present. The Kali Mas followed a different course from its present one; according to the Trawulan inscription of 1365 A.D. it flowed from Jeruk Legi over Trung and Bangsri to Gedang, to finally reach the present mouth. The explanation of this given by van Stein Callenfels, is that material from the Welirang volcanic mountain and the Anjasmoro Range was carried into the Brantas from the Kali Pikatan and her tributaries, in the same way that volcanic debris is swept along the Brantas from the Kelud volcano. The material carried into the Brantas from the south by the Pikatan, flowing into the Brangkal and thus northwards to reach the Brantas, was deposited, fan-shape, over the terrain thus steadily raising its level, forcing the Kali Mas against the foothills and directing the Kali Porong to flow from the west southwards. By the time of the Trawulan inscription the build-up of sand had blocked the previous course to Segodogang, Tulangan and Pamotan, and displaced the branching of the Kali Mas and the Kali Porong back to Mojokerto.[49]

---

[48] Significantly, the break in the river bank at Waringin Sapta (Pitu) coincided with the earliest known Kelud eruption of 1000 A.D. (see van Stein Callenfels and van Vuuren, 79).

[49] Van Stein Callenfels and van Vuuren, 80.

The waters of the Kali Konto, a Brantas tributary flowing from the Kelud mountain, were used for irrigation as early as the ninth century. The Hariñjing inscription of 804 A.D.[50] records the building of a dam and a conduit on the Hariñjing, a tributary of the Konto. In 921 A.D. this irrigation installation was reconfirmed as a freehold by the ruler Tulodong, in favour of the descendants of the original founders of the dam and the excavated conduit.[51] Near Kandangan, on the Kali Konto, a few kilometres from the inlet dam of the present major hydraulic work, the Srinjing conduit, is an inscribed stone of 1350 A.D., recording the restoration of the original dam of 804 A.D. which 'was now so solidly re-inforced that it would last for ever, for all the inhabitants of the valley east of Daha' (Kediri).[52] Unfortunately, this was not to be: the dam was washed away many times over the centuries. Even today this remains a problem area for hyraulic engineers.[53] That control of the Kali Konto has posed problems for modern engineers is indicative of the extent of the achievements of irrigation engineers in ancient Java in their efforts to control and use the waters of the Brantas and Konto, and the Pikatan, Kromong and Landean Rivers. The fact that they succeeded in harnessing these often turbulent rivers even for a time is impressive.

---

[50] Dated 784 A.D. according to P.V. van Stein Callenfels, 'De inscriptie van Sukabumi', *MKAW-L*, LXVIII, 1934, 116.

[51] Hariñjing B inscription (van Stein Callenfels, 117).

[52] P.V. van Stein Callenfels, 'De inscriptie van Kandangan', *TBG*, LVIII, 1919, 359.

[53] Attention is drawn to the modern hydraulic works in progress, the Projek Selorejo, at the headwaters of the Kali Konto. See *Kunthi*, 3, Th.II, Sapar 1903, 18.

PRINCIPLES OF IRRIGATION USED IN ANCIENT JAVA

Large scale hydraulic works can be divided into two categories: 1) those for *productive purposes* using either terrace irrigation, where rainwater run-off is directed through flumes or conduits from one level to the next, or river or stream water which is controlled and conserved in dams or artificial lakes and from there is directed through canals or conduits to the fields to be irrigated; and 2) those for *protective purposes* where, for example, floodwaters threaten certain points along the course of seasonably turbulent rivers thus placing great stress on the river banks, the powerful river flow can be controlled by barrages or retaining walls which modify the volume of water surging past the weak river bends. While serving a protective purpose these dams can also serve a productive purpose, as reservoirs from which water can be diverted into diversion dams and irrigation conduits to ditches and channels leading to the fields under cultivation.

Archaeologists have uncovered remains of impressive irrigation works of the past in China, India, Mesopotamia (Iraq), Central America, Ceylon (Sri Lanka), Israel and Egypt. In Southeast Asia there is evidence of extensive water works in Burma, South Thailand and especially in Cambodia, where traces of the achievements of ancient Angkor remain. Unfortunately, less evidence is available concerning the existence of what may have been extensive hydraulic works in ancient Java. It is clear that in Java farmers of the early centuries of the Christian era, and possibly earlier, were familiar with the basic science of irrigation and later during the Indo-Javanese period, this science was developed to a comparatively high degree of efficiency. Early evidence of flood-control is found in

King Pūrṇavarman's inscription of the fifth century, recording the excavation of a channel to divert the Kali Cakung in West Java from its northwards direction.[54] In Central and East Java remains of ancient dams and traces of tunnel work, and the spider's web of old channels and ditches spreading out over areas long since fallen into unproductivity, point to the existence of an organized irrigation system in those areas.

As far as we can determine from the available sources the methods used in ancient Java to control and conserve water for agricultural use ranged from simple constructions of weirs and dikes across small rivers and streams, erected by farmers, using bamboo, stones and tree trunks, to great stone dams, bridges or causeways, and sluices, constructed by the ruler and his legion of workers. The smaller projects, managed at village level by the farmers themselves, were more easily damaged or destroyed by floodwaters, necessitating constant repairs or rebuilding; the ruler had more manpower and resources at his command to build larger and more permanent irrigation works. The two levels of irrigation technology, however, existed side by side during the entire Indo-Javanese period.

The terminology of irrigation

Daṇuhan: The term *daṇuhan*, dam, probably applied to reservoirs, diversion dams and other means of water conservation on a large scale. Irrigation projects at this level were constructed at the ruler's

---

[54] The Tugu rock inscription of the fifth century. See J. Ph. Vogel, 'The Earliest Sanskrit Inscriptions of Java', *POD*, I 1925, 30. See also J. Noorduyn and H.Th. Verstappen, 'Pūrṇavarman's river-works near Tugu', *BKI*, CXXVIII, 1972, 298-307.

command and the supervision of such installations was in the hands of the king's rural representative for such projects. However, inscriptions reveal that the irrigation engineers and officials who carried out the actual work of building and maintaining the dam, as well as taking charge of the water distribution from these dams, were experts from the village, not from the *kraton*.

The term *dawuhan* is used in several royal edicts, the contents of which clearly indicate that the dam was part of a royal irrigation project, requiring the deployment of a large force of manpower. An example of such a construction is found in an inscription of 1037 A.D. recording the building of a *dawuhan* and a *tambak*.[55] Apart from this inscription, issued by King Airlangga, only two others actually record the building of a *dawuhan*,[56] but several other edicts refer to the reinforcement of such dams, and to regulations concerning the upkeep of dams which had been created freehold.[57] We do not know the dimensions of these dams: they are not recorded by the Javanese, as the Indian, Burmese or Cambodian inscribers recorded the measurements of similar projects. However, Maclaine Pont refers to one reservoir in the Pikatan area with the comparatively large dimensions of 175

---

[55] The Kĕlagyan inscription of 1037 A.D. (OJO LXI) lines 10-12. Work involved on such projects would have constituted *buat haji*, service to the king.

[56] The Hariñjing A inscription records the building of a dam and a canal; the Bakalan inscription of 934 A.D. records the building of three dams.

[57] Such as the Hariñjing B of 921 A.D., the Kandangan stone of 1350 A.D. and the Trailokyapuri inscriptions of 1486 A.D. (OJO XCIV-XCV).

metres by 350 metres and estimates that the dam must have held a volume of approximately 350,000 cubic metres of water.[58]

Dams were also used for defence purposes in certain developed areas in ancient times. Located outside the city limits, they could be opened to allow the water to inundate the access roads to the city, thus holding back the approaching enemy. Maclaine Pont draws attention to the fact that, not only was old Majapahit city strategically sited against a backdrop of rugged terrain, the Anjasmoro Ranges, intersected by Welirang *lahars*, but inner and outer defence lines protecting the northern and eastern approaches were apparently constructed as well. Part of this defence system consisted of dams sited at strategic points to allow the surrounding area to be inundated in an emergency. Maclaine Pont also found evidence that outside the city defence lines in the southeast the terrain appears to have been artificially dissected by man-made ravines which could be flooded by opening the dams in the area and thereby narrowing the access route of advancing troops, thus weakening their assult by forcing them to become divided into smaller units. Within the inner city defence line there appears to be evidence that a temple was situated where it could be inundated so that an enemy who may have succeeded in penetrating the outer defences could only reach the inner city with difficulty. Canals also seem to have been included in the defence system of Majapahit.[59]

What appear to be similar ancient defence systems have been found in Arakan and other parts of Burma where extensive use of water

---

[58] H. Maclaine Pont, 'Eenige oudheidkundige gegevens omtrent de Middeleeuwschen bevloeingstoestand van de zoo-genaamde "woeste gronden van de Lieden van Trik" ', *OV*, 1926, 110.

[59] Maclaine Pont, 106, 116-19.

was carried out in times past.[60] Although cities could be defended in this manner, on the other hand, an advancing army could attack both the city and the entire kingdom at one blow, by damaging or destroying the irrigation system and thus rendering useless the surrounding agricultural land, on which the city's population depended. The wellbeing of the *kraton* city depended on the smooth running of the surrounding irrigated farmland. Ruthless vandalism or the natural disasters mentioned above could bring about partial or even total destruction of a thriving agrarian centre. Such disasters undoubtedly occurred periodically in ancient times and may explain the eclipse of certain once prosperous kingdoms in Java.[61]

Dams built by the farmers across streams and smaller rivers would have been similar to the simple constructions of the present day, consisting of the material to hand such as bamboo, trunks of coconut-palms and stones. Often baskets of woven bamboo, filled with heavy stones, are used to dam smaller streams; if there are very large stones in the vicinity these are simply built up across the river. Where larger dams are required two tree-trunks are laid across the river and the space between the trunks filled with reeds, bushes, leaves and stones, with an opening left at the side as a *prise d'eau*. From here the water is directed through bamboo pipes or open channels to smaller ones from which the *sawahs* are irrigated. The disadvantages of these simple constructions lie in the fact that

---

[60] See Daw Thin Kyi, 'Arakanese Capitals: a Preliminary Survey of Their Geographical Siting', *Journal of the Burma Research Society*, LIII, 2, Dec. 1970.

[61] Concerning wilful destruction of irrigation works see V.E. Korn, *Het adatrecht van Bali*, 1924, 480. Gunawardhana writes of similar offences in ancient India. (R.A.L. Gunawardhana, 'Irrigation and Hydraulic Society in Ancient and Early Medieval Ceylon', paper presented at the 28th Congress of Orientalists, Canberra, 1971, 12.).

they are easily washed out in times of heavy rainfall or, even if the
dam holds, the floodwaters may escape through the outlet pipe and
inundate the *sawahs*. On the other hand, for small-scale farming, the
simple constructions of rock and bamboo may not be as impractical as
they seem. They are inexpensive to make and comparatively easy to
repair, an important factor when flooding comes at the height of the
rice-growing season, when repairs must be effected quickly.

Wuatan (or *wwatan*): Of the three ḍawuhan built by Rakryān
Mangibil two were named Wuatan Wulas and Wuatan Tamya. A *wuatan*
appears to be the retaining wall of a dam used as a bridge or
causeway. Juynboll gives the translation bridge but Sutjipto
Wirjosuparto translates the word as reservoir.[62] De Casparis, when
referring to the *hulu wuatan*, considers him to have been the
supervisor of bridges.[63]

Tambak (or *tamwak*): The word *tambak* occurs frequently in Old
Javanese inscriptions and appears to apply not only to smaller dams
but to dikes, tanks and ponds. Juynboll gives the meaning dam wall,
fish-pond or flood-gate.[64] In three Balinese inscriptions, written
in Old Javanese, from the years 962, 975 and 1022 A.D. where the
word *tambak* occurs Goris translates it as dike wall, wall and river
bank respectively.[65] According to Pigeaud, by the fourteenth
century the term applied to ponds or tanks for fish breeding.[66] De

---

[62] H.H. Juynboll, *Oudjavaansch-Nederlandsche woordenlijst*, 1923, 562; Sutjipto Wirjosuparto, 72-3.

[63] J.G. de Casparis, *Selected Inscriptions from the 7th to the 9th Century A.D.*, 1956, 216, note 23.

[64] Juynboll, 232.

[65] Roelof Goris, *Prasasti Bali* I, 1954, (inscription numbers 205, 209 and 352) and *Prasasti Bali*, II, 316.

[66] Pigeaud, IV, 450 (Karang Bogĕm charter).

Casparis defines *tambak* as a dam across a river, designed to create a lake, which would ensure an adequate supply of water during the dry season and ensure protection against flooding at the beginning of the wet season. The *tambak* wall would have required constant surveillance in order to regulate the outlet of water and to carry out repairs where necessary. The lake itself would also require constant care, either to deepen or to dredge it from time to time against silting.[67] Silting must have been an ever-present problem in ancient irrigation systems, particularly in lake or pond conservation works.[68]

The word *tambak* was also used as part of a place-name, for example in Tambakrejo. Similar examples are found in Talang Air (water pipes), Wuatan Mas (golden bridge), Air Manik (or *er* or *jha* as in Ermanik or Jemanik). Place-names such as these, denoting the presence of water occur, in Balinese inscriptions as well. If a study were to be made of the distribution of such place-names it may suggest that these particular areas were once important irrigation centres.

The term *tambaka* (*tamwaka*) was used in relation to dam building. In the Old Javanese metrical inscription of 856 A.D. the phrase *tamwaka ta istaka* occurs, which de Casparis translates as 'bricks to become a *tamwak*'.[69] In the Old Javanese *Rāmāyaṇa*, de Casparis

---

[67] De Casparis, II, 241, note 185.

[68] See Maclaine Pont, 125, for evidence of silting in ancient irrigation works in the Kali Pikatan area, Also V. Venkayya, 'Irrigation in Southern India in Ancient Times', *Archaeological Survey of India, 1903-04*, 1906, concerning silting in irrigation tanks in ancient India.

[69] De Casparis, 303, and note 90, (inscription XI, line 14, p.313).

further notes, the word *tamwaka* occurs, in the phrase *mangatĕra parwata len watu tambaka*, which de Casparis in this case interprets as 'to carry mountains and rocks for the dam'.[70]

Tameng (and *tamya*): There is very little reference to this term. Kromodjojo Adi Negoro refers to *tameng* as a dike and reports that at the place named Tameng on the Kali Pikatan he found ruins of an ancient dam.[71] Maclaine Pont also refers to 'enormous rock layers' he found at Tameng, which he considered to be the remains of Wuatan Tamya, one of the dams built by the Rakryān Mangibil.[72]

Suwak: Originally the term probably applied to *sawah* fields and the earthen walls around the fields, to contain the water. In Old Balinese inscriptions referring to the irrigation associations, the term *kĕsuwakan* is used,[73] (modern, *subak*). In New Javanese *suwakan* refers to the banked-up edges of a small pond on the side of a river, for the purpose of trapping fish.[74] The present-day term for small dikes in rice fields is *galengan*. The term also applies to the earthen walls of *sawah tadahan*, terraced fields dependant on rainwater, and to the walls of irrigation channels running through *sawah sorotan*, irrigated fields. The term *suwakan* or *kĕsuwakan* has not been found in Old Javanese inscriptions but *subaki* occurs in the Trailokyapuri inscription of 1486 A.D. and has been translated by van

---

[70] De Casparis, 322, note 49.

[71] R.A.A. Kromodjojo Adi Negoro, *Oud-Javaansch Oorkonde*, I, 1921, 14, note 5.

[72] Maclaine Pont, 124-5.

[73] See Goris, I, 23 (Klungkung inscription).

[74] P. Jansz, *Practisch Javaansch Nederlandsch woordenboek*, 1913, 863.

Stein Callenfels as the place-name Subaki, one of the villages sharing irrigation water in the Penanggungan region.[75]

Talang: There are occurrences of the word *talang* in Old Javanese records but it is only used in place-names, such as Talang Air or Talangan. *Talang* are open pipes or small aquaducts, usually of bamboo, used for irrigation purposes. There is very little available information concerning *talang* in Old Javanese sources but the term is still in use. They may have served a similar use as the Ilocano *aripit* (small pipe).[76]

Wĕluran: This term refers to conduits or irrigation channels. Reference is made in the Bakalan inscription to the flow of irrigation water along the irrigation channels, the *wĕluran* (in Bahasa Indonesia, *saluran*). The equivalent term in Balinese appears to be *tlabah*. It is not known whether canals were also known as *wĕluran* or whether there is another Old Javanese term not yet recognized. In Ilocano large conduits or canals are known as *kali*.[77] In the Hariñjing inscription the phrase *qawainira kali i hariñjing*[78] occurs, which refers to the original Hariñjing conduit, now the Srinjing conduit.

Arung: In Bali the term for tunnel is *aungan*, derived from *arung*.[79] In the Old Balanese inscriptions, Bebetin A of 896 A.D.[80] and the Batuan

---

[75] P.V. van Stein Callenfels, 'Bijdragen tot de Topographie van Oost Java in de Middeleeuwen II' *OV*, 1926, 83.

[76] Lewis, 144, note 2.

[77] Lewis.

[78] Van Stein Callenfels, 'Sukabumi inscription', 16, line 4.

[79] J.L. Swellengrebel, Introduction, *Bali: Studies in Life, Thought and Ritual*, 1960, 11. See also F.A. Liefrinck, *Bali en Lombok*, 1927, 83.

[80] Goris, I, 55 (Bebetin AI, IIb, line 1).

of 1022 A.D., [81] *undagi pangarung*, tunnel builders, are mentioned along with other craftsmen and skilled workers (*undagi*). Swellengrebel remarks that if there were tunnel builders in Bali as early as 896 A.D. 'it may be assumed that wet-rice farming on Bali is significantly older than that'.[82] As yet, no reference to *arung*, or a word which may designate irrigation tunnels in ancient Java has been found but the New Javanese term for tunnel is *urung*.[83] As the two Balinese inscriptions mentioned above were written in Old Javanese this fact may point to the possibility that tunnel building was also carried out for agricultural purposes in ancient Java at a very early period. There is archaeological evidence in Java pointing to the existence of tunnel-work for irrigation use but no date has been given to these remnants. The *Encyclopedia of the Netherlands Indies* states that in various places in Java 'covered waterworks' (tunnels) of the Indo-Javanese period have been found embedded in *padas*. During the flood of 1861, when the Kragilan conduit in the Regency of Purwarejo was destroyed, an ancient underground channel was uncovered. According to the Encyclopedia this covered channel is considered to date from the 'Buddhist' period.[84] Unfortunately, the Encyclopedia does not give the source of this supposition or any further details.

Maclaine Pont refers to tunnels he found in the region of old Majapahit and notes that in the city layout itself a tunnel seems to have been used to direct water from a small river to flow through the temple complex which, in Maclaine Pont's opinion, could have easily

---

[81] Goris II, 169 (Batuan, IIIa, line 1).

[82] Swellengrebel, 11.

[83] Jansz, 1184.

[84] *Encyclopaedië van Nederlansch-Indië*, I, A-G, 1917, under the subject 'Bevloeing' (irrigation) 89-90.

been inundated for defence purposes.[85] Other tunnel remnants were found by Maclaine Pont and his colleagues, one of which is still used to conduct water from the Slawe dam near the confluence of the Pikatan and Kromong Rivers to *sawah* fields nearby. According to Maclaine Pont's report there are at least eight other water tunnels or remnants of them, to be found in the region. He refers to tunnel remnants at Tameng, Wates and Pandan and describes a ruined tunnel which he considers was constructed to direct irrigation water northwards from the Kali Pikatan area to the drier Penanggungan region. This underground irrigation channel is estimated by Maclaine Pont to have been two and a half metres in width and three metres in height, and to have been cut through hard *padas*.[86]

Tambuku: Three Balinese inscriptions, written in Old Javanese, refer to a *tambuku* in connection with *sawah* cultivation. Goris translates the word as distribution block.[87] In Bali at the present day the distribution block is known as a *tembuku* or *temuku*. Made from concrete or wood, usually the latter, the *tembuku* consists of a beam with two or more notches at the top, placed across the main conduit at a point where irrigation water is to be directed into secondary channels and ditches.[88] According to Dutch writers of the previous century a *tembuku* or distribution block was not used in Java in their time. Gorkom, however, notes that the Javanese rice farmers did have

---

[85] Maclaine Pont, 119.

[86] Maclaine Pont, 121-8.

[87] Goris II, 317 (Glossary). *Tambuku* is mentioned in inscriptions numbered 436, 438 and 1008.

[88] See C.J. Grader, 'The Irrigation System of Jĕmbrana', *Bali: Studies in Life, Thought, and Ritual*, 273, and 387, note 4. See also F.A. Liefrinck, 'Rice Cultivation in Northern Bali', *Bali: Further Studies in Life, Thought, and Ritual*, 58-9.

a certain means of allocating water to each *sawah*; the men spoke of 'one, two or more feet of water' which, Gorkom says, applied to the volume of water. The speed of flow was not taken into consideration.[89] Lekkerkerker also remarks that the Javanese farmers, unlike the Balinese who use a distribution device, work by the 'feel' or by estimation of what is a fair and just amount of water required by each farmer.[90] Jay writes, with regard to the present-day Javanese *sawah* cultivators, that water is apportioned to each farmer according to the size of his fields, by two methods of estimating the quantity required, neither method employing a *tembuku*. The first method is known as *jam-jaman*, 'measured by the clock', the second method is *maren-marenan*, 'to sufficiency'.[91] Although there appears to be no apparatus such as the *tembuku* used in Java it seems significant that this means of allocating each farmer's or each group of farmers share of irrigation water should be known as a *tembuku* in Bali, a word stemming no doubt from the old Javanese word *tambuku*. It is possible that this is an indication, however tenuous, that some Old Javanese methods and techniques of irrigation farming fell into disuse while yet continuing to exist in Bali.

Rice cultivation

The type of soil and the topography of the area to be brought under cultivation determine the type of rice cultivation. There are two

---

[89] See K.W. Gorkom, 'Het water op Java, in betrekking tot den landbouw', *Indische Gids*, I, 1, 1879, 559-60. Gorkom recounts that while living in the inland agrarian regions for years he had frequently found that suddenly the entire area was drained dry, due to a farmer having blocked off the irrigation water-supply or drawn it off for his own use. No one seemed to know of any means of redress for such anti-social acts.

[90] Lekkerkerker, 532-3.

[91] Robert Jay, *Javanese Villagers*, 1969, 333-7. Jay describes the two methods of allocating water in the foregoing pages.

methods of cultivation, dry-field and wet-field, both of which are referred to in Old Javanese inscriptions. 1) *Dry-field cultivation:* in ancient Java this method was referred to as *tĕgal* and *gaga*. *Tĕgal* land mainly refers to unterraced fields or fields on open plains or flat ground: the term remains in use to the present. (*Tĕgal* land is not considered as valuable an asset as *sawah* land). *Gaga*, a term also in use at present, (gogo), refers to permanent unterraced dry fields on hilly slopes or in the mountains. They are less intensively cultivated than *tĕgal* land but more intensively so than *ladang* (swidden). Unlike *ladang, gaga* is permanent farmland. *Gaga* is mentioned in charters, as well as *sawah* and *rĕnĕk*.[92]

There are references in inscriptions to changes having been made from *tĕgal* cultivation to *sawah* cultivation,[93] which we may take as an indication of the extension of an existing irrigation system in the neighbourhood, where the *tĕgal* land would have been required as extra acreage for *sawah*. 2) *Wet-field cultivation*: where rice during the course of many centuries became adapted to growing in water, cultivation on a more intensive scale could be carried out, on land dependant on rain-water run-off or by means of artificial irrigation. This is known as *sawah* cultivation in Indonesia, and the rice grown in *sawahs* is referred to as *padi*. Fields dependant on rain-water are *sawah tadahan*, hillside terraces. Fields which are irrigated by directing water through pipes, ditches and channels to flow over the fields under cultivation, are known as *sawah sorotan*. Inscriptions reveal that in ancient Java rice was also cultivated in morass or swampland and known as *rĕnĕk* or *rawa*. Both Siṇḍok and

---

[92] For example, in OJO LXI, line 4 there is reference to *gaga* and *rĕnĕk*.

[93] The Ngabean II inscription of 879 A.D., OJO 12, line a:2.

Airlangga appear to have carried out reclamation in the marshes along the Brantas delta; according to Airlangga's Kĕlagyan inscription, produce from rĕnĕk land was also liable for tahil, taxation.[94]

Little is known about agricultural tools used for *sawah* cultivation in ancient Java. There are references in several inscriptions to certain implements which were presented as gifts at foundation ceremonies, some of which cannot be translated. Others include iron tools such as an adze, crowbar, pick-axe, mattock, chisel and a chopper-knife.[95] The fact that these iron implements were symbolically presented to the sacred foundation stone is an indication of the high value placed on items made from iron at that time. Although not mentioned in inscriptions, there are two agricultural implements used for *sawah* cultivation which have survived since Neolithic times until the present day, the *pacul*, hoe, and the *ani-ani*, reaping knife.

The *pacul* is a broad flat hoe with a straight cutting edge, used in the soft wet soil of the *sawah* fields. The *ani-ani* has a wide distribution in Southeast Asia and known under various names. Like the *pacul* it has a very long history in Java but is now giving way to the *sabit*, the sickle. The *ani-ani* has a flat blade of about 5-7 cm., attached to a wooden handle by a wooden pin. The rice, which is cut in the direction in which it bends, is drawn towards the knife-blade and the rice-stalks are swiftly severed, several at a time. The reaper proceeds until he has a handful, which is called an *agem*. Five *agems* are bound together to form a sheaf, a *pencar*. Fast workers can cut 10-12 *pencars* per day.

---

[94] OJO LXI, line 4

[95] J.G. de Casparis, *Inscripties uit de Çailendra-tijd*, 1950, 48. (Karangtĕngah) and Sarkar, I, 222 (Ngabean II, B.I, lines 8-9).

Land and water measurements

The earliest (indirect) reference to surveyed land is found in the Plumpungan inscription of 752 A.D., wherein it is recorded that a piece of ground was made over as a 'gift to the god' to become the village of Hampra.[96] The earliest record of actual measurements used for agricultural land appears in an inscription of fifty-seven years later, the Dieng stone of 809 A.D.[97] Three measurements used specifically for *sawah* land in ancient Java are referred to, i.e. the *lamwit*, the *tampah* and *blah* (*bĕlah*, half) and reference is made to the surveying or 'marking out' of the land for *sawah* fields. Most Old Javanese inscriptions give evidence that fields intended for *sawah* cultivation were carefully measured and the measurements recorded.

Land marked out at the instigation of the ruler or a high court dignitary for the purpose of establishing freehold *sawah* land was recorded permanently, on stone or copper plates; records would first have been made on *lontar* leaves and afterwards committed to stone. Records of the surveying of villages and the farmlands of the farmers when they cleared and settled on the land would have been committed to *lontar* leaves and kept in the village or hamlet. In the case of a *sīma* grant of *sawah* land the surveying or measuring out was always 'witnessed' by representatives from the neighbouring villages, the *tpi sering*, whose land bordered on the newly surveyed land. The surveying of land seems to have been carried out by a high-ranking official, such as a *nāyaka*,[98] where *sīma* land was concerned, and in

---

[96] De Casparis, I, 9-11.

[97] Sarkar, I, 49.

[98] According to Sarkar I, 109, note 79, the *nāyaka*, who had an administrative position, had a definite say in land surveying, as evidenced in the Palĕpangan inscription (Sarkar II, 57,

many inscriptions it is recorded that a *raka* or *rakryān*, or priest, arranged the 'marking out' of the land, but it was usually a *samĕgat* who carried out this work. Boundaries were usually identified by natural landmarks such as rivers, hills or mountains. Stone columns were also used as 'boundary pegs', sometimes inscribed with a record of the status of the land, if the land happened to have been awarded freehold rights. The boundaries of neighbouring *sawahs* were strictly observed and where a freehold estate adjoined peasant land a 'fence' of bamboo, a *walĕr*, was erected or a *sawi* used, a demarcation cord of fibre and bamboo poles with streamers attached, which is still in use to the present.[99]

In ancient Java two methods of measuring *sawah* fields were in use, the lineal measurement and measurement by volume. These measurements are still used in rural areas. The first method was apparently used when virgin land was cleared and surveyed for the cultivation of wet rice (which is referred to as *manusuk sīma lmah*) and evidence for it is found as early as the Dieng stone of 809 A.D. An area measurement used frequently in Old Javanese inscriptions is the *tampah*, which seems to have been used especially to define the size of *sawah* fields. The *tampah* is first mentioned in the Dieng stone,[100] and in subsequent records appears to have been used in

---

[98] (contd)
lines 2-4). Sollewijn Gelpke in his report on government redistribution of agricultural land in Java in the nineteenth century, notes that the village head did not survey the land; this was done by the *penjarikan*, scribe. (Sollewijn Gelpke, 'Het desabestuur op Java. Een bijdrage tot de kennis van Land en Volk', *De Indische Gids*, I, 1, 1879, 284.

[99] According to Pigeaud entrance to an estate which has a *sawi* suspended over the road or pathway is forbidden. (Pigeaud IV, 460). See Pigeaud III, 176 concerning land measurements.

[100] Sarkar I, 50-1. See also the Palĕpangan inscription and de Casparis, II, 316.

connection with *sawah* land which was freehold, for the income of temples and other *sīma* property. The area of such *sawah* land seems to have ranged between 2 and 6 *tampahs*. However, it seems that two *tampah* measurements were in use, one of which it could be said was a standard *tampah* and the other a royal *tampah*, *tampah haji*. Sarkar suggests that the second measurement was probably introduced to avoid possible disputes or abuses in surveying,[101] such as had occurred and been recorded in the Palĕpangan inscription of 906 A.D. According to this inscription a *tampah haji*, the measurement used to re-survey the *rāmas*' land, was 100 *dĕpa sihwa* in length by 30 *dĕpa sihwa* in breadth.[102]

A *dĕpa* according to Liefrinck,[103] is the span of a man's outstretched arms, approximately two metres. A Balinese measure, a *dĕpa agung*, appears to be a square measure equalling one *paceraken*, or nine square metres. The Old Javanese *dĕpa* appears to have been used from very early times until the fifteenth century where large tracts of land were involved. In the Śri Manggala inscription of 874 A.D.[104] the *panĕgat* of Hino marked out a freehold for his own funerary temple,

---

[101] Sarkar II, 59, note 18.

[102] *Tampah haji sātus dpa sihwā pañjangnya singkrēnnya tlung puluḥ dpa* (Sarkar II, 56, line 5 [Palĕpangan]). A difference of opinion between the *rāmas* of Palĕpangan and the *nāyaka* Bhagawanta is recorded, concerning the size of the *rāmas*' *sawah* fields, for which they had to pay six silver *dharana*, more than they could afford. The *rakryān mapatih* Hino agreed to their request to have their fields re-measured according to the 'royal' *tampah*, which reduced the overall total 'acreage' while the tax assessment remained the same.

[103] F.A. Liefrinck, 'Rice Cultivation in Northern Bali', *Bali: Further Studies in Life, Thought, and Ritual*, 1969, 54.

[104] Sarkar, I, 195 and II, A1, line 2.

measuring 44 ḍĕpa by 67 ḍĕpa. The Ngabean I copper plates record the surveying of 'extensive lands' for a freehold domain measuring 72 ḍĕpa by 63 ḍĕpa. In the Suradakan Charter of 1447 A.D.,[105] the ḍĕpa is the only measurement referred to in the record of the size of the extensive freehold domain grounds. Thus, it seems as if a ḍĕpa applied when large tracts of land were involved and a ḍĕpa sihwa was used in connection with sawah fields for farmers or for garden land.

A term in connection with rural land measurements, but whose precise value is not known, is the *katik*, which in inscriptions usually follows the measurements *lamwit* or *tampah*, for example, 'the *sawah* fields under the united body of the *tajis* to be taken care of by the *rāmas* measured 6 *lamwit*, 3 *tampah* and 28 *katik*.'[106] The term *lirih* also occurs in old records and is interpreted by Pigeaud as a *sawah* measurement, probably originally meaning 'track'.[107] Other area measurements are the *lattir* and the *barih*. In the Wanua Tĕngah inscription of 863 A.D. the *barih* occurs as 'the *sawah* land of Kasugihan measures 3 *barih* yielding 1 *hamat*'.[108] (for *hamat*, see below). According to de Casparis a *barih* equalled six *lattir*.[109] Unfortunately it is not yet possible to give a precise equivalent for all measures.

Measurements were taken by the limbs of an average man, one of the farmers. *Tangan*, for example, is the length between the lower arm

---

[105] Muhammad Yamin, 11-13.

[106] OJO XXVI, lines 5-6.

[107] Pigeaud III, 153 and IV, 397. See also F.H. van Naerssen, *Oudjavaansche Oorkonden in Duitsche en Deensche Verzamelingen*, 1941, 73 (Inscription VI).

[108] Wanuah Tengah II, line 3 (Sarkar, I, 180). See also de Casparis, I, 72.

[109] De Casparis, I, 59.

and the tip of the middle finger, which seems to compare with the
Balinese measurement *siku*, reported to be based on the distance
between the elbow and the tip of the outstretched middle finger. Other
smaller Balinese measurements are *langkat*, the span of an outstretched
thumb and middle finger and *depa*, the span of a man's outstretched arms.
The *bahu (bau)* is a standard Indonesian measurement today, equivalent
to approximately 1 3/4 acres; the original meaning of *bahu* signified
a man's 'strength', his shoulder and upper arm. One wonders whether
originally it could have represented the amount of produce from a
certain acreage that could be carried by one man. Four *bahus*
equalled one *jung*, or seven acres, and one *kikil* equalled half a *jung*,
3 1/2 acres.[110] The *jung* is referred to quite early in Old Javanese
epigraphy.[111] From ancient times the rice yield from a certain area
of *sawah* land was the basis for fixing land tax. In Java a piece of
land producing sufficient rice for one family was known, for purposes
of taxation, as a *karya* or 'farmer's field'. Five *karyas* amounted to
one *jung* for taxation estimates; the *jung*, being a complex of *karyas*,
was probably a more practical measurement to use when estimating the
amount of tax to be paid, or for estimating the size of an estate.
However, the *jung*, consisting of five *karyas* is an equivalent from
later times; it may have consisted of a lesser number of *karyas* in
earlier times.[112]

The second method used for measuring *sawah* fields, by volume
estimates, appears in inscriptions recording a change in ownership of

---

[110] The *kikil* occurs in the Karang Bogĕm charter of 1387 A.D. (Pigeaud IV, 450).

[111] Van Naerssen, 73, note 6.

[112] According to Gericke and Roorda the *karya* equalled a *bahu*. See J.F.C. Gericke and T. Roorda, *Javaansch-Nederlansch handwoordenboek*, 1901, 436, column 2 and 462, column 1.

sawah land already established, which was to become a freehold property either by gift or deed of sale. The size of the field already under cultivation was given according to the amount of rice grain it was estimated to produce, and this amount was expressed in a unit of weight called a *hamat*,[113] the weight of the rice. Through long experience the farmer knew how much seed grain would be required to produce a certain yield from a *sawah* field of a certain size. The field was said to have a yield of, for example, 8 *hamats* - *sawah winihnya hamat 8*.[114] In the Karangtĕngah inscription of 824 A.D., concerning the gift of *sawah* lands by Raka Patapan and his wife, the size of the fields, five in all, are expressed by their *hamat* yield. '... the grounds of Kayumwungan, their yield was 1 *hamat* 1 *wha*.' ($1^{1}/2$ hamat).[115]

In Java, as in Bali, the *tĕnah* was a volume measurement used to estimate the production capacity of *sawah* fields of varying size. The *tĕnah* measurement is still used in Bali, not only to express an estimate of the yield of a certain field but also to express the volume of irrigation water required for the field. To quote Birkelbach:

> *Tĕnah* is a term Balinese use to establish land productivity via an input-output formula. A *tĕnah* is a variable unit which relates water, land, rice seedlings planted and harvested

---

[113] The unit *hamat* is still used; it first appears as a unit of measure in the Karangtĕngah inscription of 824 A.D. and therefore gives some evidence of the antiquity of *sawah* cultivation in Java.

[114] See the Śri Kahulunan II inscription (de Casparis, I, 86, 91.).

[115] Karangtĕngah inscription, line B27, ... *winihnya ha 1 wha 1* ..., de Casparis, I, 40. According to de Casparis the word *wha* is probably an abbreviation of *wĕlah*, half, and *ha(mat)*. (See de Casparis, 48, note 6.)

> yield. A *těnah* of water is the amount of water
> needed to irrigate a *těnah* of land to its
> optium growing level. A *těnah* of land produced
> a relatively fixed amount of *padi* from a
> variable number of seedlings.[116]

The term *těnah winih* is applied to a certain area planted with a quantity of rice seed, the normal amount for a certain number of rice sheaves. *Těnah* also appears to represent an area measurement consisting of 800 *pacěraken* of nine metres each, i.e. 1 *těnah* = 7,200 square metres.

THE BALINESE SEKAHA SUBAK

Sekaha subaks, irrigation associations, have existed in Bali for centuries but the system appears to have been unknown elsewhere in Indonesia in recent times. According to Korn similar organizations are to be found only in Madagascar and in the Philippines, in Northern Luzon.[117] The Ilocano of Northern Luzon have irrigation guilds which are called *pasayak*, but it is not known whether these date from pre-Spanish times, although Lewis considers it likely; all technical and operational terms are in Ilocano not Spanish.[118]

The purpose of this section is to provide a closer look at the *subak* system in Bali in the event that it may give some indication as to whether a similar organization of irrigation management existed in

---

[116] Aubrey N. Birkelbach, Jr. 'The Subak Association', *Indonesia*, 16, Oct. 1973, 155, note 3.

[117] V.E. Korn, *Het adatrecht van Bali*, 1924, 47.

[118] H.E. Lewis, *Ilocano Rice Farmers. A comparative study of two Philippine barrios*, 1971, 133, 144. Lewis remarks that the head of the *pasayak* is known as the *pangulu*, which is similar to the Old Javanese title for irrigation official, *pangulu bañu*.

Java prior to the close of the Indo-Javanese period. As we have noted in the Introduction to the present work writers of the turn of the century were surprised to find no traces of an indigenous system of hydraulic organization to compare with the Balinese *subaks*, although they considered that such a system was likely to have existed in Java in earlier times.

There is evidence that in Bali *subak* systems were in operation at least three centuries before the Majapahit era in Java. Inscriptions issued in 1022 A.D. by Anak Wungśu, the younger brother of the East Javanese ruler Airlangga, refer to *kĕsuwakan*. These inscriptions make particular reference to *sawah* land within a *subak* complex, the *sawah Kaḍangan i kĕsuwakan Rawas*.[119] Unfortunately, there are no similar references found in Old Javanese epigraphy, although this need not lead to a negative conclusion regarding the likely existence of similar guilds, independent of village administration, in ancient Java. *Suwak* is an Old Javanese term for a dike or earthen wall around a *sawah* field. So far the word has only been found to occur in the Trailokyapuri inscription of 1486 A.D. but it has been read as a place-name, Subaki, by van Stein Callenfels.[120] It is contended here however that the word probably refers to a *suwak*, especially in view of the fact that the inscription concerns detailed irrigation regulations.

The Balinese *subak* consists of a complex of individually owned *sawah* fields receiving water from the same irrigation system, either from a major conduit or through a network of smaller channels.[121]

---

[119] Roelof Goris, *Prasasti Bali*, I, 1954, 23, (Klungkung A and B).

[120] Van Stein Callenfels, referred to on p.32 (OJO XCV, b, 4, 7).

[121] See C.J. Grader, 'The Irrigation System in the Region of Jĕmbrana', *Bali: Studies in Life, Thought, and Ritual*, 1960, 276-88; and Aubrey Birkelback Jr., 'The Subak Associations', *Indonesia*, 16, 1973, 153-69 for present day *subak* activities.

All phases of irrigation administration and cultivation within the *sawah* complex are carried out by the farmers themselves, as members of a *sekaha subak*, an irrigation association. The basis of the *subak* system is its complete independence of village administration. Although the farmers have certain obligations to their village, all matters pertaining to their rice fields, such as the planting and harvesting arrangements, water distribution, maintaining and policing the irrigation installations, finance and religious obligations, in fact all facets of irrigation farming, come under the sole responsibility of the *sekaha subak* of each particular *sawah* complex. The *sekaha subaks* play a very significant part in the rural life of Bali. The advantages of belonging to such an association include not only its material benefit to the farmers, as a group as well as individually, but social and religious enrichment as well. Membership, generally of no more than a hundred members, strengthens the social ties existing between farmers, who not only work in close co-operation but meet regularly at *subak* meetings.

As Balinese *subaks* have always been closely concerned with both ground and water rights, fixed rules and regulations, strictly adhered to, have applied to both since early times. Groothoff maintains that the Balinese *subak* system developed as an entirely indigenous Balinese concept, due not only to the Balinese inherent spirit of co-operation but also as a natural development arising from ground and water rights which he considered to be peculiar to Bali.[122] Such rules and regulations pertaining to ground and water rights were laid down by

---

[122] A. Groothoff, 'Studie over het inlandsche waterschapwezen (soebakwezen) op Bali en Lombok', *Adatrechtbundel*, 15, 1918, 372. Groothoff regarded Balinese land and water rights as unique.

subak officials, in consultation with all members of the *subaks* in less important areas and by the ruler in key regions. Records of land and water rights and regulations pertaining to agricultural management were carefully preserved, becoming part of the sacred collection of *kertas* referred to in the Introduction above. Van Eck and Liefrinck point out that there were formerly two kinds of village and *subak* regulations: 1) *awig-awig*, laws and regulations transmitted orally at village level; and 2) *kerta sima*, rules and regulations issued by the ruler and kept in the *kraton* archives.[123] *Kerta sima subak* are a type of *praśasti*, a charter or edict, recording the setting out of a new *sawah* land and the foundation ceremonies and feasts held to mark the occasion.

The majority of *kerta sima subak* begin by recording a newly formed *subak* association, or by defining the borders wherein a particular *sekaha subak* was to exercise control. Then follow explicit rules and regulations which apply to every *subak* member, from those of the *brahmin* caste to the lowliest *sudra*.[124] Members are urged to live in peace and harmony with each other and with neighbouring *subak* members with whom they share the irrigation water, to work diligently and to choose a *klian subak*, a head, with care, having regard to the attributes required of a *subak* head. The *klians* themselves were instructed to maintain good relations with the village administration and to weigh

---

[123] See R. van Eck and F.A. Liefrinck, 'Kerta-sima of Gemeente en Waterschappenwetten op Bali', *TBG*, XXIII, 1876, 161-5.

[124] It is an accepted fact in Bali that where agriculture is concerned no privileges are accorded to rank or caste. Liefrinck remarks that no one, however high his caste, was ashamed to take part in rice cultivation. A *brahmin* never minded being asked to repair a water conduit or to work with spade in hand by the side of a *sudra*, who as a fellow *subak* member was his equal. (F.A. Liefrinck, 'De Rijstcultuur op Bali', *De Indische Gids*, II, 2, 1886, 1054). See Birkelbach for the place of the *brahmin* caste within *subak* associations of today (Birkelbach, 157).

all questions and complaints by *subak* members without bias or favour. They were also to see that the rules regarding offerings to be made to the agricultural deities were performed faithfully, whether the harvest happened to be a good one or a failure. Further regulations contained in *kerta sima subaks* concern the organization of the *subak*, rules for various duties to be fulfilled, the *klians'* obligations to members and vice versa, as well as regulations concerning water distribution, taxes, fines, and the conducting of religious feasts and yearly *subak* cock-fights.

Subak officials

At the present time the three government officials connected with *subaks* are the *sedahan agung*, the *klian sedahan* and the *sedahan tambaku* (nowadays *sedahan tembuki* or *sedahan jeh*). In pre-Colonial times these three offices were part of the court structure. The *sedahan agung*, the district head, was accountable only to the ruler. This office appears to be the equivalent of *pembekel* or *punggawa* in Java. The *klian sedahan* is the link, as it were, between the *sedahan agung* and the *sedahan tembaku*. The *sedahan tembaku* has charge of all *subaks* within the boundaries of one village, or within the territory covered by several villages situated close together. They pass on to the *subak* heads any instructions from government level issued through the *sedahan agung*. They also decide on the allotment of irrigation water to each *subak*, where several *subaks* are drawing water from the one source.[125] Birkelbach considers that the present function of the *sedahan tambaku* or *sedahan jeh*, as tax collector for the Indonesian

---

[125] F.A. Liefrinck, 'Rice Cultivation in Northern Bali', *Bali: Further Studies in Life, Thought, and Ritual*, 1961, 11f.

government and also as liaison officer between the government and the farmers, is essentially the same as in pre-Dutch times.[126]

The *klian subak* is the permanent head of the *sekaha subak*, assisted by his *juru arah*, scribes or criers, who are chosen by him with the other *subak* members' approval. In pre-Dutch times there were assistants at a lower level known as *sayas*. The *pekasih* are those *subak* members who perform, in turn, duties such as repairs to dikes and conduits or the construction of new small-scale conduit systems. The *pemangku*, the *subak* priest, holds a semi-official position within the *sekaha subak*. He is responsible for the care and maintenance of the *subak* temple. He supervises any repairs to the temple and performs the dedication of offerings made by *subak* members and their families to the *subak* deities and guardian spirits of dams and irrigation systems.

Forming a subak

Whenever a new *subak* is to be established the preliminary organization is carried out by one of the group of farmers who have decided to form the association. The man chosen is the one considered most competent to supervise the initial work of laying down the irrigation system, i.e. excavating the conduits and so on. He must be a man with outstanding ability in organizing a work force and he must be honest in handling the finance necessary for the new irrigation project. When the initial work of establishing the new *sawah* area is complete, the leader steps down and a meeting is held to choose the *klian subak*, the permanent head. A *kerta sima subak* from Buleleng, said

---

[126] Birbelbach, 160.

to be extremely old, instructs the *subak* members to choose a *klian* with care.[127] When the choice has been made - and it is often the man who has just stepped down - a report is drawn up for the *sedahan tambaku*, who passes it on to the *sedahan agung* for his approval.

The position of *klian subak* is an onerous one which calls for a man of impeccable character and one who has had sufficient education to enable him to read and write. He must not at the time hold a position within the village administration nor within the temple, and he must not be childless - as adult men without children take second place in a basically agrarian society. He should also be experienced in wet-rice farming and water distribution, and he is expected to be able to represent the *sekaha subak* in dealings with village officials and with the *sedahan agung*. He must strive to maintain good relations with both. His duties are extensive and demanding, as every facet of irrigation work is under his direct control. He also supervises the regulation of water allowance to each *subak* member's fields, although this is done in close consultation with all members of the association.

The *klian subak's* first duty in a newly formed *sekaha subak* is to draw up a *sawah* register, a *pipil* or *pemarik*, a collection of *lontar* leaves on which is recorded the names of every *sawah* owner, his address and the size of his rice fields, for tax purposes. Of interest here is the report in Eindresumé II,[128] which states that in Pasuruhan, in East

---

[127] When staying in a village in Jembrana in 1976 the author was shown a collection of *subak* regulations by the *klian subak*. These regulations, although written in Bahasa Indonesia, had obviously been passed down for generations.

[128] *Eindresumé van het onderzoek naar de rechten van den Inlander op den grond*, II, 253, quoted by Liefrinck, 'De Rijstcultuur', 1043, note 1, concerning an investigation into ground rights for the landowners of Java and Madura.

Java, the use of a *pipil*, given out by the village head was noted, on which was recorded the names of the *sawah* owners, the size of their fields, the amount of tax payable and so on.

Subak duties

Subak members, in pre-colonial and early colonial times, were expected to fulfil the following duties:

1) those directly affecting the *subak* and the members; and

2) those duties ordered by the ruler, to be carried out by *subak* members for the ruler's benefit, and for the benefit of the state in general. To the first category belong the following duties, as set down in *kerta simas*;

1. *Maintenance of dams, conduits and sluices*, and the making of ponds and other smaller irrigation works.

2. *Guarding the conduits and the irrigation water* supply. Regulations state that irrigation installations containing only a limited quantity of water shall, as soon as the water level becomes low, be guarded day and night by a number of *subak* members, to prevent fishing or damage to the installations and particularly to prevent stealing of precious water by *sawah* owners further downstream. The *klian subak* must personally check that the guards attend to their duties.

3. *Maintenance of roads and culverts*. Roads that are used by the *sekaha subak* must be maintained by the members. These roads, which are open to the public, are used by *subak* members when transporting their harvested rice to the rice barns, and by their womenfolk, who pass to and fro to the *subak* temple to present their offerings. Culverts must be maintained where the irrigation conduits cross a roadway.

4. *Police surveillance within the subak*.

5. *Construction and maintenance of the subak meeting house and temple*. No *subak* association is without a temple wherein the agricultural deities are worshipped and called upon to protect and ensure the fertility of the rice fields.

The second category, that of service to the ruler, includes maintenance of the *kraton*, which was carried out jointly by the *subak* members and other villagers. The *subak* members were expected to provide raw materials such as straw for wall linings, *atap* for roofing and firewood and cooking ingredients for the kitchen.[129]

Water regulations

In Bali the ruler, as earthly representative of the gods 'owned' all water flowing naturally, therefore his right to tax the rice yield hinged on his indirect right to the water flowing in the rivers and larger streams, used for irrigating the farmers' *sawah* fields. Van Eck and Liefrinck observed that the water tax, *suwinih*, was considered by the people to be a small fixed fee for which the ruler 'hired' river water to his subjects: they, by paying *suwinih* to the ruler, were making an offering to the river god.[130]

The ruler delegated the responsibility for irrigation management at court level to his representative, the *sedahan agung*. The *sedahan agung* in turn entrusted to the *sedahan tambaku* the duties of water distribution to the *subak* complexes. At the *subak* level, distribution to individual fields was in the hands of the *klian subak*. Conversely, in the case of dam construction, if members of a newly established *sekaha subak* wished to site their dam on a river where dams already existed they had first to obtain the ruler's permission by appealing through their *klian subak* to the *sedahan tambaku*, who in turn passed the appeal to the *sedahan agung*. The *sedahan agung*, being the ruler's representative, commenced action by first investigating the site to ensure that the dam would not be too close to existing dams, thus

---

[129] See Liefrinck, 'Rice Cultivation', 19-24.

[130] R. van Eck and F.A. Liefrinck, 'Vertaling van de Kerta Sima Subak of waterschappenwetten', *TBG*, XXIII, 1876, 216. Also Groothoff, 315f.

possibly affecting the water supply of the established *subaks*. After these *subak* groups have signified their agreement to share the water source, the river with the new *subak*, permission is granted to construct the new dam.

It is also determined at the time of building the dam how much water will be allowed to the new *subak* in times of low water level, and in which month they will receive their share of water from the river. From then on the new *subak* members are free to dispose of their joint share of irrigation water amongst themselves, providing that they observe the rules of water restrictions in times of drought, and providing that they pay their *suwinih* to the ruler. The Gede *kerta sima subak*, number 108,[131] provides an example of regulations which apply to a group of *subaks* sharing the same water source. Regulations for water distribution between the Gede *subak* and three others include instructions stipulating the width of the opening of the main conduit, to ensure that each *subak* in its turn receives the allotted amount of irrigation water. The size of the opening is expressed in *tampahs*. The *kerta sima* also records that ten *tembukus*, distribution blocks, were in use in the main conduit to divert the water to secondary channels.

Fines and penalties

According to Liefrinck, guarding *subak* property was a duty of the highest importance. Very heavy penalties were imposed on members who had transgressed the laws laid down in *kerta sima subaks*. Damage to *sawahs* or to dike walls caused by someone's animals, for example, led

---

[131] Groothoff, 347. The first few pages of this *kerta sima* are written entirely in Old Javanese.

to severe punishment for the owner. Some *subak* regulations contain directions concerning guard duty, in order to protect the *sawah* from damage or to discourage theft from the rice crop. Fines imposed were to be paid by the following *subak* monthly meeting, otherwise the fine was to be doubled and the farmer given three days in which to pay. If he still failed to settle the fine the fact was brought to everyone's attention by the placing of a bamboo pole, with dry leaves and a bundle of straw attached, in the transgressor's *sawah*, and at the same time cutting off his irrigation water supply. The farmer is given a further three days in which to settle his fine; during this time his fields are mortgaged for the amount of the fine, often to the *sedahan* himself.[132]

Infringement of any *sekaha subak* rules was dealt with at the monthly meeting. Those who refused to submit to assembly decisions were fined. Before this occurs, however, the recalcitrant member has a right to present his case to the *sedahan tembaku*, or to the *sedahan agung*. In *kerta sima subaks* fines are stipulated for loss of work animals, the stealing of *padi* and *bibit*, and other offences such as fishing in the irrigation channels, also the compensation fee or impost payable to the farmer over whose land another lays his irrigation pipes. Water stealing appears to have been the most heavily punishable crime, in both Java and Bali.

The first part of the Bakalan inscription, issued by Rakryān Mangibil of East Java in 934 A.D., contains parallels to be found in Balinese *subak* regulations, which leads one to surmise that the edict may have been a *kerta sima subak*. As we have mentioned on page 44, a *kerta sima subak* is a type of *praśasti* or edict recording the

---

[132] Liefrinck, 'De Rijstcultuur', 1056-8.

establishment of new *sawahs* or a newly formed *subak* association and includes rules and regulations for the members' guidance. The Bakalan decree was directed to the *rāmas* of five villages situated along the Pikatan River, most of them still in existence. The Rakryān's directive concerns the use of three dams which she had constructed for her people. Regulations concerning the use of the irrigation system are stipulated and the *rāmas* are instructed to see that the farmers are fully aware of the significance of the regulations, and that they abide by the rules applying to water distribution. There is also a prohibition against fishing from the channels.[133]

Three officials are mentioned in the inscription, the *samĕgats* Susuhan and Taplan and Punta Pakatuppan. The *samĕgats* may have fulfilled duties in the capacity of '*sedahan agung*' and '*sedahan tembaku*', the court officials connected with *subaks* referred to on page 45. Punta Pakatuppan, who was responsible for the irrigation installation may have been the '*klian subak*' of the area.

---

[133] According to Korn (*Het Adatrecht van Bali*, 476, 479) the villagers were free to fish in the channels providing care was taken not to cause damage to the rice plants. Fishing in the irrigation channels at night was forbidden, as it was in the Bakalan charter. The Bakalan prohibition could have applied to a certain period of the year, to allow for fishbreeding. Sutjipto Wirjosuparto ('Apa sebabnya', 72) suggests that not only were Rakryān Mangibil's dams to be used for irrigation purposes but for fishbreeding as well. The Sundanese charter of Cri Jayabhupati in 1030 A.D. forbids fishing near the sanctuary (Pleyte, 'Maharaja Cri Jayabhupati' *TBG*, LVII, 206).

CHAPTER TWO

SAWAH CULTIVATION AT VILLAGE LEVEL

Van Naerssen maintains that even before the adoption of Indian principles of kingship and court administration in Java a dual social structure already existed, consisting of villages governed by *rāmas* and a council of elders, and a centralized administration headed by a *raka*. The former functioned as producers and the latter as distributors of produce and services, with an equilibrium of power between them, adjusted to mutual needs.[1] A system of irrigation management involving mutual co-operation between several villages dependent on the same water source required a leader who could command authority not only in his own village but over all the villages working in co-operation. Thus, there arose the concept of rulership, or *raka*ship.

Raka is apparently a title of great antiquity. According to Pigeaud the term for ruler, *raka* (or *ratu*) and *haji* have their counterparts in kindred languages of the Indonesian archipelago, which indicates a very early concept of indigenous rulership.[2] Van Naerssen remarks that, although it can only be surmised, the *raka* was probably chosen from among the *rāmas* of the villages involved in mutual co-operation, to become the 'older brother' among them, which is the original meaning of the term *raka*.[3] The earliest *raka*ship, thus,

---

[1] F.H. van Naerssen, 'Twee Koperen Oorkonden van Balitung in het Koloniaal Instituut te Amsterdam Holland', *BKI*, XCV, 1937, 447.

[2] Th. Pigeaud, *Java in the 14th Century*, IV, 1962, 470.

[3] F.H. Naerssen, 'Some Aspects of the Hindu-Javanese Kraton', *Journal of the Oriental Society of Australia*, II, 1, 1963, 17.

was a pre-Indianized institution, arising from the need for an authoritative leader as *sawah* cultivation increased and villages began to combine to share their agricultural activities. The *raka's* position of authority steadily increased during the Indo-Javanese period, from that of paramount chief to one of more centralized power and influence and in many cases to that of supreme rulership. This will be discussed in the following chapter concerning the *mahārāja* and his *kraton* administration.

Throughout Indonesia's long history of economic and cultural development the basic unit, the village, has remained a stable core in the centre of surrounding change that occurs with the passing of time. Van Vollenhoven, in his monumental work on Indonesian *adat*, refers to what he calls the 'old style' village of Java, unchanged since remote times.[4] These early autonomous settlements consisted of a single village unit or a village with an attached hamlet, a *dukuh*, which may be likened to small islands, surrounded by their *sawah* fields and gardens. As the population increased more land was brought under cultivation and in this way settlements began spreading over the land. In time, since the hamlet had its own border delineation it could become a separate village while still adhering to the *adat* of the mother village, eventually to attain independent status. Such agrarian expansion continued throughout the Indo-Javanese period and is clearly evident in inscriptions, for example in the numerous records of land surveys and the evidence of duplication of place-names.

---

[4] C. van Vollenhoven, *Het adatrecht van Nederlansch-Indië*, I, 1931, 513. See also J.H.F. Sollewijn Gelpe, 'Het desabestuur op Java. Een bijdrage tot de kennis van Land en Volk', *De Indische Gids*, I, 2, 1879, 136.

Each village was governed by its own *adat*, through a council of elders, the *tuha wanua*, presided over by one of their number, a *rāma*, who was considered not to be above his fellow elders but 'first among the equals'. The villagers were known as *anak wanua*, 'children' of the village; the farmers in particular were *anak thāni*, 'children' of the *thāni*, the cultivated land. Each village possessed its own communal work animals and so on. Land, water and buildings were under joint care, and the communal needs of each village could be provided by the mutual assistance of the people within its borders. The village, in short, was a small self-supporting community living as one close-knit family, the basic family unit within the larger familial community structure, the village as a whole. However, as more land was brought under *sawah* cultivation it became increasingly necessary for neighbouring villages to combine their efforts and to share the available water supply and labour.

Van Akkeren, writing of ancient Javanese village societies, remarks that:

> Wet-rice cultivation encourages very much all activities directed at restraining the wild forces of nature; it stimulates the population to achieve a high degree of mutual co-operation and aid; peace must be maintained with neighbouring villages. Technical ability, organizational skill, special care for the preservation of social peace and the harmonious development of the community and the other social virtues have in the course of two or three thousand years formed the special character of the Javanese people ... in Java the village evolved as an autonomous institution, on the one hand, in dependence on co-operation with neighbouring villages in the irrigation area, on jurisdiction, etc., and in some cases on the rulers, but on the other hand, in loyalty to its own autonomy and organization.[5]

---

[5] Philip van Akkeren, *Sri and Christ*, 1970, 5.

VILLAGE ORGANIZATION

There appear to have been three types of village structure in ancient Java during the Indo-Javanese period, and probably earlier.

1. *The nuclear village*, the *wanua*, with autonomous administration.

2. *A federation of villages*, the *mancapat* and *mancalima*, bound by common interests such as the construction and maintenance of irrigation systems, and mutual defence. Intervillage administration would only have operated for these specific purposes.

3. *Regional village communities*, probably *karamān*, (in the fourteenth century, *dapur*), with each village possessing autonomy, under its own *rāma*, but all being subdivisions of a larger community structure, with its own boundaries.

Living within the *wanua* were three classes of villagers: those who possessed *sawah* land and their own house or compound; those who owned a house only, perhaps with some *tĕgal* land but not *sawah*; and those without property.

The owners of *sawah* fields, the free farmers or core villagers as Dutch writers designate them, being descendants of the original village founders who had cleared the land and laid out the first *sawah* fields in the area, were the village 'elite', known as the *anak thāni* or *kulina*. This exclusive membership was passed down from father to son, or other legitimate heir where there was no son to inherit the *sawah*.[6] The *anak thāni* must always have been a closed class, enjoying full rights and privileges from the earliest times.[7] Even today *sawah* owners are considered to possess higher status than *tegal* owners. Within this class of free farmers were the *sawah* owners who had

---

[6] There is evidence that women owned land in their own right. See Chapter Three, pp. 92-4.

[7] Van Vollenhoven, I, 527f.

retired and handed over their farmlands to their heirs during their own lifetime. These older men, the *kaki*, 'grandfathers', continued to play an important role in village affairs as advisers on matters of *adat*.

The second group, those villagers without the status of *sawah* ownership, were, in the previous century and at present, home owners whose house was on someone else's land. Farmers of *tegal* fields are included in this group. In modern times they enjoy only partial rights and privileges. Nowadays widows and elderly invalids are included in this category but it is not known where these people belonged within the social scheme of the ancient Javanese village. They are probably mentioned in inscriptions but as so many Old Javanese terms are still obscure they cannot be identified.

The third group of villagers, those without property, at the present time includes unmarried children of *sawah* owners, newly married couples and newcomers to the village. These people have no rights and privileges at all. It is not known what their status would have been in ancient Javanese society. Children are mentioned in inscriptions as being present at foundation ceremonies, and even receiving ceremonial gifts, but they would have been children of village dignitaries.

There were bondmen living within the rural communities, as farm labourers and servants. Many of them may have been farmers who had mortgaged their land and been unable to redeem it or who had fallen into debt to their masters for some other reason. However, little is known about this group of people; some probably worked for the free farmers in their fields and others for the members of the aristocracy on religious domains and estates.

Wet-rice cultivation demands a well-organized irrigation management and Indonesian farmers in the developing *sawah* areas early learnt to adjust their pattern of life in accordance with these demands. Agricultural techniques, ritual and philosophical outlook were all closely interwoven and adjusted to a special cosmological pattern of daily life. The Javanese and the Balinese arranged their entire social system in relation to the cosmic classification of the four cardinal directions and the centre. This classification they also applied to their rural organization.

The cosmic concept was manifest in the grouping of four villages around the mother village, situated according to the points north, south, east and west, with the core village in the centre. Inscriptions reveal this system of village grouping whenever reference is made to the *rāma tpi sering*, the *rāmas* from the neighbouring villages who attended a village ceremony. The villages are mentioned in clockwise order. Pigeaud suggests that the Biluluk charter contains a possible key to ancient village organization in its reference to the social structure of four clans plus an outside clan.[8] It may be possible that this fifth clan was represented by the as yet unidentified *kalima*, mentioned in inscriptions concerning village gatherings.[9] The grouping of five villages was known as the *mancapat*. Kartahadikoesomo writes that there are places where the old *mancapat* system is still preserved, and in certain regions the system has been revived for the purpose of solving present irrigation problems.[10] Generally speaking

---

[8] Pigeaud, IV, 420-21 (Biluluk charter).

[9] See W.F. Stutterheim, 'Inscriptie op een zuiltje van Papringan', *TBG*, 1933, 96-101. Stutterheim suggests that the *kalima* was the equivalent to the *pengliman* of Bali, assistant to the *sedahan*, and fulfilling duties as *subak* police.

[10] Soetardjo Kartahadikoesomo, *Desa*, 1953, 66.

however, the old *mancapat* system of co-operation among villages for irrigation management no longer exists. Van Akkeren considers that with the introduction of administrative divisions and subdivisions introduced by the Netherlands colonial government, the *mancapat* system was destroyed.[11]

There is evidence from as early as the ninth century A.D. that the *mancapat* village grouping was, in some areas, extended to the cosmic classification of eight compass directions plus the centre. This village grouping was known as the *mancalima*, whereby eight villages were clustered around the central village in a concentric grouping of the four cardinal points and the four intermediary points. In a Central Javanese inscription of 842 A.D., an even wider village complex is recorded, consisting of twenty-four villages grouped in concentric fashion, representing the eight points multiplied by three symbolizing, de Casparis suggests, the three worlds, heaven, earth and the underworld. In this extended village complex the central unit was a religious domain instead of the core village.[12]

The third group of village organizations mentioned above, the regional communities, Pigeaud considers to represent the oldest form of territorial organization of rural communities. Each village was free and independent within the larger structure. These communities were probably the *karamān*, the lands of the *rāma deśa*, the 'fathers' or leaders of the district, and the *sawah* owners, the *kulinas*. In

---

[11] Van Akkeren, 7. Van Akkeren considers that there must have been irrigation co-operatives in ancient Java.

[12] See J.G. de Casparis, *Inscripties uit de Çailendra-tijd*, 1950, 150-51. De Casparis includes a chart of the Mantyāsih domain on p.159.

the fourteenth century these were known as *ḍapurs* but Pigeaud considers it possible that the *ḍapurs* and the *karamān* were the same.[13] However, unfortunately, very little is known of either. Apart from the regional agricultural communities of *rāmas* and *kulinas* the various religious communities held land in agrarian regions. Also outside the city limits were the appanages or estates belonging to the aristocracy. These are discussed in the following chapter.

VILLAGE BUREAUCRACY

Old Javanese inscriptions give evidence of a highly organized village bureaucracy. Judging by the large number of village authorities and minor officials listed in many of the inscriptions there appear to have been many degrees of rank. The largest group of officials mentioned in the charters, always at the end of the list of officials present, following the court representatives, belongs to the village administration; in the Perot inscription there are about nineteen different officials listed among the villagers at the ceremony recorded.[14] Sarkar, discussing both court and village officials, remarks:

> The most interesting, if not surprising, thing in respect of these official titles is that their number is very large and the majority of them are non-Indian and non-Sanskritic. The titles of rājā, mahārāja, mantrī, mahāmantrī, pati(h), bhagavanta, likhitapatra, nāyaka, variga and perhaps one or two others are of Indian origin, but the overwhelming majority of the titles are of Indonesian or Austronesian origin. This implies that before the arrival of the Indians in Java, the original population of Central

---

13 Pigeaud, 301 and 495.

14 See J.G. de Casparis, *Selected Inscriptions from the 7th to the 9th Century A.D.*, 211-43, concerning the Perot inscriptions.

> Java [and East Java] had a political organization,
> whose origin cannot be satisfactorily traced at
> present, but if the meanings of these Old-Javanese
> titles be any guide they seem to point to a well-
> regulated tribal organization, in which the
> officials had a distinct role to play. Apparently
> the fine distinction of officials belonging
> to similar categories and having similar
> significance - e.g. *tuha* (n), *juru, rama,* etc.
> who are apparently some kind of village-chiefs
> or elders - is hard to determine at present,
> but the multiplicity of village officials itself
> indicates that there existed a tribal
> organization of efficient type in the villages.[15]

Prominent among the various officials mentioned in inscriptions are several whose specific function was connected with irrigation. These officials appear quite early in Old Javanese epigraphy. Among the irrigation officials mentioned are the *matamwak*, the *hulu wuatan* and the *hulair* or *huler* (the latter term being a contraction of *hulu-air* and *hulu-er*). The function of the *matamwak* was probably that of a village elder in charge of irrigation installations such as the construction of dams and artificial lakes or other conservation works.[16] The term, derived from *tamwak (tambak)* occurs fairly frequently in inscriptions. Other references in connection with the word *tambak* are *patih tambak*, for example the head of the Princess of Lasĕm's fisheries mentioned in the Karang Bogĕm charter.[17] There are also the titles *mpu tamwak* and *matamwak mula* (perhaps a dam surveyor) appearing in inscriptions. In the Candi Perot inscription

---

[15] H.B. Sarkar, *Corpus of the Inscriptions of Java*, I, 1972, xix. See also H.B. Sarkar, 'Survey of Some Aspects of Old-Javanese Inscriptions of Central Java', in Buddha Prakash (*ed.*), *Studies in Asian History and Culture*, 1970, 48-9. Sarkar draws attention to the strong pre-Indian tribal organization of the village during the Indo-Javanese period.

[16] See de Casparis, II, 230.

[17] Pigeaud, IV, 451.

is the phrase ... *si layar matawak si tamuy mula* ... which de Casparis translates as ' ... Si Layar; the surveyor of the dams: Si Tamuy; the *mula* ...' De Casparis observes here that the term *mula* is not clear but probably refers to someone connected with irrigation.[18] The word *mula* occurs elsewhere in connection with irrigation, for example in the Hariñjing A inscription it is used in relation to a dam and a canal, ' ... *bhagawanta bari i wulaggi sumsaksyakan simaniran mula dawuhan gawainira kali i hariñjing* ...'[19] which can be read as 'the priests Bari of Wulaggi, in the presence of witnesses, confirmed their good works, (or foundation), the dam and the Hariñjing canal (artificial river) ...'. It is not clear, however, whether *mula* applies to the *sīma* or to a certain kind of dam. For the present *mula* must remain untranslated.

There are many references in inscriptions to the official called *hulu wuatan*. The term occurs early in inscriptions and in no less than seven between the years 863 A.D. - 918 A.D.[20] The *hulu wuatan* was probably an engineer supervising the construction of bridges and causeways. Together with the *hulair* this official seems to have occupied an important place in the agricultural community. Stutterheim refers to the *hulu wuatan* as a bridge supervisor.[21]

The *hulair* appears to have been an irrigation official of some standing in ancient Java. In several inscriptions he follows immediately after the *tuha wanua*, a senior village elder, and the

---

18   De Casparis, II, 241 and note 186.

19   P.V. van Stein Callenfels, 'De inscriptie van Sukabumi', *MKAW-L*, LXXVIII, 1934, 116.

20   L.C. Damais, *Repertoire Onomastique de l'Epigraphie Javanaise*, 1970, 116-17.

21   W.F. Stutterheim, 96-101.

wariga, the village astrologer, who held an important place in village affairs. There may be some significance in the words found in the Palĕpangan inscription concerning the three men. ... *nahan kweḥ nira mangagam kon* ...[22] 'now all of them, having powers to pass orders ...'. According to de Casparis the *hulair* was probably in charge of the maintenance of the irrigation system, including the distribution of the irrigation water supply to the *sawahs*.[23] It is possible that the *hulair* could have performed the same function as the *klian subak* of Bali. In several inscriptions, recording the presence of village officials, both secular and religious, at the *sīma* foundation ceremony, the *hulair* was the only official connected with irrigation to be included among those witnessing the occasion. In some inscriptions two *hulairs* are mentioned together in attendance at the ceremonial function. The term *hulair karamān* also occurs in some inscriptions and seems to indicate a council of irrigation heads.

Closely connected with the *hulair* is another term frequently mentioned in inscriptions, the *pangulu bañu*, a term over which scholars are not entirely in agreement. Van Naerssen considers *pangulu bañu* to be probably a later form of *hulair* and translates both as 'head of the irrigation system' (*hoofd van de irrigatie*).[24] De Casparis also considers the *pangulu bañu* and the *hulair* to be the same irrigation official.[25] Stutterheim writing of the Papringin inscription of 882 A.D., in which the *hulair* and the *hulu wuatan* appear together,

---

[22] For example, in the Palĕpangan inscription of 906 A.D. (Sarkar, II, 57, lines 14-15) Sarkar points out that these three had executive functions (59, note 32).

[23] De Casparis, II, 230.

[24] F.H. van Naerssen, *Oudjavaansche Oorkonden in Duitsche en Deensche Verzamelingen*, 1941, 50, note 5.

[25] De Casparis, II, 241, note 184.

suggests that the *hulair* had the same function as present-day *ulu-ulu*, officials who maintain the irrigation system.[26] Pigeaud, on the other hand, considers *pangulu bañu* to signify 'irrigation-water retribution' where the term occurs in the Sarwadharma charter.[27] In one of the Trailokyapuri inscriptions the phrase *pangulu bañu pisis 8400* ...[28] appears, which could perhaps be taken to mean 'water payment (levy) of 8400 *pisis*'. However, some two centuries earlier the ruler Kĕrtanagara issued a charter wherein is stipulated the various amounts to be contributed by the villagers of the area where the source of the irrigation water was located, towards the upkeep of the previous king's sanctuary. Van Naerssen translates the phrase as 'the head of the irrigation must pay 1 *mā sū*, 9 *mā* and 1 *ku*'.[29] The term *bañu*, as also *air*, *er* and *jha*, means water. However, it has been noted that wherever the word *bañu* appears in inscriptions it applies to irrigation water, or is mentioned in connection with *sawah* cultivation. *Pangulu* is usually translated as 'head' or supervisor. It appears then that the translation of *pangulu bañu* as 'supervisor of the irrigation system' might be more acceptable than in connection with payments for water. The term is still used at the present time (*pengulu banu*) and applies to an irrigation inspector, or supervisor of the irrigation works.

---

[26] Stutterheim, 100, note 2.

[27] Pigeaud, IV, 383, 387; Pigeaud, III (plate 3, recto, line 2). By the term 'retribution' Pigeaud is referring to compensation, or an impost, payable by farmers whose source of irrigation water either flows through, or is located on, someone else's property.

[28] Trailokyapuri inscription, OJO XCV, lines 8-10, for example.

[29] Van Naerssen, 46 and 48, line 3, ... *pangulu bañu, mā sū* 1, *mā* 9, *ku* 1 ....

An irrigation official referred to in Balinese inscriptions written in Old Javanese, is the *nāyaka air*, which Goris translates as 'supervisor of the irrigation water supply'.[30] As *nāyakas* were usually court officials, or officials under the *rakryāns* in ancient Java, the *nāyaka air* may have been the equivalent of the present-day *sedahan tembuku* in Bali, the government (in former times, court) official connected with the *subak* associations. Also connected with *sawah* cultivation in ancient times was the *hulu wras*, according to de Casparis probably the official in charge of the communal rice supplies. De Casparis remarks that the *hulu wras* is often mentioned with the *rāmas*. He also notes that van Vollenhoven referred to similar functionaries in the villages of his time and concluded that the office dated from recent times.[31] However, van Vollenhoven's observation appears to be incorrect. In ancient Javanese society the *hulu wras* seems to have been an official of some importance; in the Kamalagi inscription of 821 A.D., for example, he follows the *hyang guru, dapunta* Dahana, an ecclesiastical person, and he precedes the various *patihs* mentioned in the list of witnesses to the foundation of freehold *sawah* land and gardens.[32] In view of the apparent importance of this village official it may be possible that his function was more than that of being in charge of the village rice (*wras*) supply. He may have also been in charge of rice supplies for export.

---

[30] Roelof Goris, *Prasasti Bali*, II, 278.

[31] De Casparis, 243, note 205.

[32] Kamalagi Inscription, Recto, lines 9-11 (Sarkar I, 58).

LAND AND WATER RIGHTS

A certain amount of supposition must be used where the study of ancient Javanese land and water rights is concerned. Pigeaud's work on the Majapahit period is of great value for an insight into conditions existing in the fourteenth century. By using this information together with Old Javanese inscriptions it is possible to reach some tentative conclusions concerning the earlier Indo-Javanese period. T.C. Lekkerkerker maintains that the Indians upon their arrival in Java early in the Christian era found a purely Javanese rural organization, with indigenous land rights already laid down.[33] Van Vollenhoven remarks that in the Kedu region in Central Java, in the original 'core' areas or free lands, he found that the old *adat* concerning land rights was still remembered.[34]

The right to occupy virgin land stemmed from the act of clearing the forest or uncultivated land. This right corresponds to the rights of possession of running water which the act of laying down irrigation pipes gave. Cleared virgin land was known as *bakalan* (*bakal*, to clear, to begin). *Individual ownership* rights applied to a single pioneer farmer; when he had cleared new ground he was given three years in which to develop and establish *sawah* fields before he became liable to tax payments. The clearing of land and the establishing of *sawah* fields by several farmers together led to *joint ownership*. If the entire population of a village worked together to establish fields for the mutual benefit of every member of the community the land was held in *collective ownership* as village

---

[33] T.C. Lekkerkerker, *Hindoe-Recht in Indonesië*, 1918, 31.

[34] Van Vollenhoven, I, 604.

sawah. Exemption from tax for the three years it took to develop the land probably applied in all cases. There appears to have been a limit set on the amount of individual land holding, as in Bali, in order that *sawah* land did not fall into too few hands. In Bali a ruling was enforced on the maxium number of *sawah* fields any one farmer may own, in order to ensure that the possession of agricultural land did not fall into the hands of a minority. A farmer could not exceed the maximum 'acreage'; if he did so the amount of land in excess of his permitted holding had to be given to a farmer who had less than the allowed amount and the exchange was executed by a correct legal transaction.[35]

The bond existing between the farmer and the land he had himself carved from the forest was indeed deep and lasting; ownership was considered paramount, to be passed on to the next generation and the next, to be valued and tilled with care, as the soil inherited from one's own ancestors. An example of the importance placed on the right to land ownership, and the close attachment existing between the family and the land they owned, is seen in the Jaya Song *jayapattra* of about 1350 A.D.,[36] concerning a dispute between two families over ownership of an estate. The claimant in the case maintained that the estate rightfully belonged to his family, although he admitted that the land had been in the defendant's family's possession for a hundred years or more, due to the fact that his great-great-grandfather had borrowed a sum of silver from an ancestor of the defendant, giving the estate as security. The defendant, on the other

---

[35] See F.A. Liefrinck, 'De Rijstcultuur op Bali', *De Indische Gids*, VIII, 1886, 1217.

[36] Jaya Song decree, c.1350 A.D. (Pigeaud, IV, 391-8).

hand, claimed ownership by inheritance. His family, he claimed, had owned the land for seven generations but, as it dated from such a remote period of time, there was no written evidence of ownership. The defendant's claim also hinged on the antiquity of ownership, reaching back over 360 years to the tenth century, which he was able to prove to the satisfaction of the court. It seems that either written records or local knowledge (probably the latter, since the defendant's evidence consisted of the testimony of three witnesses) kept track of the ownership of land over a very long period. The fact that the plaintiff could bring forward a claim to land which he said his great-great-grandfather had in some way mortgaged or pawned a hundred years before, suggests that the consideration of *original* ownership would weigh heavily with the court.

The village head appears to have had absolute rights of disposal of agricultural land remaining unredeemed from debt, and land which had belonged to a farmer who had died without heir, also land which had been abandoned for some reason. If land was neglected or allowed to lay fallow for three years it apparently reverted to the village head. However, it is not clear whether the disposal of this land was decided by the village head alone, or whether in consultation with the village community as a whole. Land was rarely sold. Pigeaud writes that 'according to Javanese (and generally Indonesian) customary law (*adat*) selling of land was almost inconceivable: the owner and his land were so closely bound up one with another that they could not be severed for ever and ever'.[37] However, there are recorded instances where in ancient times the ruler, and sometimes *rakryāns*, purchased agricultural land which they may have wished to

---

[37] Pigeaud, IV, 52.

create as a *sīma* estate or domain. In the Lintakan inscription of 919 A.D. for example, it is recorded that the ruler Tulodang purchased *sawah* land from the rāma of Kasugihan for a sum of silver, for the purpose of establishing a freehold. It is noteworthy that, although the ruler was able to clear forest areas for cultivation he was not free to appropriate *sawah* land but had to purchase for cash these established rice fields.[38] Garden land was also purchased in some instances, for example when the Rakryān of Sirikan bought for one gold *karṣa* the garden land belonging to the guild of *rāmas* of Mamali, for the purpose of making it freehold, the produce from which land would then benefit the temple of Gunung Hyang.[39]

Because it contains details in common with many Old Javanese inscriptions, of land measurements and the manner in which the exact location of *sawah* fields belonging to the various farmers was carefully recorded, the following modern example of a deed of sale of *sawah* fields is of interest. It is a deed of sale of *sawah* fields belonging to a villager of Blora in 1877 A.D.

> Ngawen, September 23d 1877.
> I, called Pak Bedru from the hamlet of Wangil, a hamlet of the village of Kendajaken, in the district of Ngawen, Blora, have sold indeed my own sawah bakalan, to the extent of 1½ bahu, divided into three parts, situated northwest of the hamlet of Wangil, in the range of fields called Tike, limited to the north by the river, to the west by the kebayan's fields, to the south by the modin's fields, to the east by the kamituwa's fields, - for fifty guilders. The sawah is bought by the man called Asnawi modin of the village of Punggurreja, in the district of Ngawen.

---

[38] Lintakan copper-plates of 919 A.D. (Sarkar, II, 170).

[39] Copper-plate of Mamali (Polengan V) of 878 A.D., lines 2-3 (Sarkar, I, 215).

The contract reads that it is performed for ever, from generation to generation. As to the land revenue, Asnawi pays it. I have received the purchase money in its entirety.

Here follows my sign:

Pak (X) Bedru

Witnesses in cognizance of the transaction:

1. Setrajaya, village chief.

2. Ranatruna, kamituwa

Known to me:

district chief of the district of Ngawen.

(s) the clerk.

(The foregoing is a quotation from an English translation published in Adatrechtbundel 33.)[40]

Except for the instances where ownership of agricultural land was relinquished by sale to another, if a farmer found himself in financial difficulties, the usual practice was to mortgage the land, which he could subsequently redeem. An inscription issued in 966 A.D. concerns the mortgaging of certain *sawah* land which was subsequently redeemed by the owner for one and a half times the mortgage price.[41] There is also a record of mortgaged land having been redeemed by other than the owner. In the second part of the Kĕmbang Arum inscription of 901 A.D., according to Sarkar's translation, it states that the Rakryān of Wantil, his wife and three sons, purchased the mortgaged land of the *rāmas* of Panggumulan, and also purchased garden land and *sawah* fields from the *dapuntas* Prabhu and Kaca for three

---

[40] *Adatrechtbundel* 33, 1930. ('Ontwerp voor een verzameling van adatoorkonden', p.16).

[41] N.J. Krom, *Hindoe-Javaansche geschiedenis*, 225.

kati of silver.[42] Bosch, in his translation of the passage, considers that the *rakryān* and his family redeemed the *rāmas'* land by handing over to the mortgager (whose identity is not disclosed) the gardens and *sawah* fields they had purchased from the two 'honourable gentlemen'.[43] A hypothetical explanation of this transaction is that the Rakryān of Wantil and his family probably wished to obtain the *rāmas'* land in order to include it in the lands in Panggumulan which they had created as a *sīma* domain for religious purposes the previous year (first part of the inscription); the *rāmas'* land may have adjoined it. The *rakryān* who is also referred to as *raka*, and his wife *dyaḥ* (princess) Prasada and their sons were in a position to redeem the mortgaged land, and to purchase the gardens and *sawah* fields as well; it would have been a pious act on the *rāmas'* part also to relinquish their land to a religious domain.

No doubt many farmers became involved in debts they were unable to meet, and in this manner they probably lost their land to someone else, who could afford to redeem it. Regulations dating from the eighteenth century in Bali may throw some light on the subject of land mortgage in ancient Java. By-laws issued by the ruler, and said to be based on ancient decrees, include the rights of both mortgager and mortgagee and rulers for the settlement of debts; the ruler's permission to mortgage land had to be obtained.[44] Share-cropping *paron* or *maron*, is another custom of ancient origin. Share-cropping

---

[42] Panggumulan I and II (Kĕmbang Arum) of 902 A.D., IIIb; lines 9-11 (Sarkar, II, 38).

[43] F.D.K. Bosch, 'De Oorkonde van Kembang Areom', *OV*, (1925), Bijl.B, 49.

[44] F.A. Liefrinck, *Landsverordeningen van Inlandsche Vorsten op Bali*, 1917, 185.

on a farmer-landlord basis involved halving the produce of a given *sawah* field. In the case of communal village land there was a five-part division of harvested produce; one-fifth to the village authorities, two-fifths to the ruler and two-fifths to the farmer who produced the crop. The *paron* system exists to the present.[45]

As far as rights to irrigation water in this period of Javanese history are concerned, there is even less evidence available than for land rights. According to observations made by Dutch writers of the nineteenth and early twentieth centuries, there did not appear to be any definite ruling on water rights during the colonial period from which we could possibly have drawn conclusions for earlier periods. There are inscriptions which give direction concerning water distribution and payment.[46] The Sarwadharma charter of 1296 A.D. contains the instructions which read, following Pigeaud's translation, 'as to the case that there is buying of (irrigation) water by the lands of those Royal servants that form their support, they shall join in the buying in accordance with (6) the irrigated rice-fields they have'.[47] Pigeaud suggests that the obligatory compensation payments for irrigation water was 'particularly effective for blackmailing purposes' during the fourteenth century; landowners downstream, if they were 'unwilling to pay up', could have their water supply cut off by neighbours further upstream.[48]

---

[45] See Soemarsaid Moertono, *State and Statecraft in Old Java*, 1968, 115f and Fukeo Ueno, 'Rural Settlements and Rice Harvest in Java from the standpoint of socio-economic Rural Geography' in R.L. Singh (*ed.*), *Rural Settlements in Monsoon Asia*, 1972, 299f.

[46] Van Naerssen, 46.

[47] Sarwadharma charter, plate 4, verso, lines 5-6 (Pigeaud, III, 147).

[48] Pigeaud, IV, 383.

Van Vollenhoven observed that in recent times the *sawah* farmer possessed the right to water flowing through his own irrigation pipes or channels. If another farmer wished to use this water he must first obtain permission from the owner of the pipes and pay for the water he used, either by cash or part of his harvested rice. There appear to have been no individual rights to the actual flow of water, i.e. whether a particular farmer should receive the first or the later flow; these rights were considered communal and could only be carried out communally. The right to his share of the irrigation water supply lapsed for anyone who did not contribute towards the carrying out of irrigation maintenance.[48]

---

[48] Van Vollenhoven, I, 632-33. Van Vollenhoven notes that in his opinion irrigation management in Java was a village concern and that irrigation associations such as the *sekaha subak* did not exist.

CHAPTER THREE

SAWAH CULTIVATION UNDER KRATON SUPERVISION

The development of *sawah* cultivation in ancient Java has been observed thus far, from its early beginnings through the growth of small village settlements practising simple irrigation farming under the administration of *rāmas*, and to the formation of village federations under the supervision of a *raka*, leading to the nucleus of a *kraton* society. With the adoption of Indian principles of divine kingship[1] and the concept of the supreme ruler, the mahārāja, the simple hydraulic technology and methods of administration employed in the earlier periods of development progressed, in certain regions of Java, to large-scale irrigation projects consisting of stone dams, bridges and canals, and eventually tunnels, which were probably in existence by at least the eighth century, under the Śailendras of Central Java and the Kañjuruhan kingdom of East Java. This development did not replace *sawah* farming on a simple scale at village level, which would have been carried on outside and independently of the more advanced agrarian regions administered under the *mahārāja*.

It is unlikely that the Javanese received their basic knowledge and techniques of irrigation management from India but the principles of kingship and priestly administration, which undoubtedly gave impetus to the development of large-scale hydraulic centres, came

---

[1] It is beyond the scope of this work to discuss all aspects of divine kingship and its application to ancient Javanese statecraft. However, there are many works dealing with the subject at length, such as B.J.O. Schrieke, *Ruler and Realm*, 1957; S. Moertono, *State and Statecraft in Old Java*, 1968; D. Weatherbee, *Aspects of the Ancient Javanese*, 1968; and K. Hall and J. Whitmore, *Explorations in early Southeast Asian history: The origins of Southeast Asian statecraft*, 1976.

from India at a time when the Javanese agricultural development was ready to pass to the florescent stage of development, if we apply Adam's and Collier's theories on the stages of development of irrigation societies.[2] Scholars are in general agreement that Java was in contact with India at least by the first century of the present era, if not earlier. The fact can be accepted that Javanese *rakas* became aware of the enhancing aspects of Indian kingship and the influence of the priesthood in strengthening the ruler's position.

In order to carry out his function effectively it was necessary for the *raka* to maintain a monopoly over the rights of disposal of labour and surplus produce, which would have resulted from more intensive rice cultivation as time went on. These rights of disposal of labour and surplus produce naturally involved sovereign authority over the federated villages of which the *raka* was paramount chieftain. The need to organize the increasing scale of production and all it entailed would have required a firm central administration. This in turn would have led to the nucleus of a court structure, centred around the *raka* presiding over his seat of authority, the early *kraton*.

Increased *sawah* cultivation would have brought with it a desire for political expansion as certain *rakas* gained greater power and influence over their neighbouring *rakas*, probably due to a greater rice yield and perhaps an increased volume of petty trade. However, an ambitious *raka* would also have been aware that his position was vulnerable; he would have been one of several competing against each other, all of similar rank. His position, therefore,

---

[2] Discussed in Chapter One, pp.6-7.

would have required strengthening and enhancing in such a way as to raise him above his fellow *rakas*, in short, to give him the status of sovereign ruler. In order to gain the desired authority over neighbouring rural areas he would have need to gain access to more agricultural land than he already presided over. It was at this point in the development of Java's embryo *sawah*-based kingdoms that the bearers of Indian culture arrived on the scene, to implement Indian-style kingship with its aura of prestige and authority. The stage was set for the appearance of the *mahārāja*, the paramount ruler.

Kingdoms arose and developed, and some waxed powerful during the centuries of the Indo-Javanese period. New organizational structures were adopted as small agrarian centres developed into Indianized principalities and kingdoms. New elements of law were introduced, borrowed from India and used side by side with the traditional *adat*.[3] Religious duties were taken over by brahmins who replaced the indigenous priests in the *kraton* centres. Here they wielded great power. *Kraton* officials, some of them adopting Sanskrit titles, gathered around the ruler who although adopting the title of *mahārāja*, the Great King, retained his *raka* title as well. Throughout the Indo-Javanese period lesser but independent rulers, *rakas* and *rakryāns*, continued to govern their own smaller territories. However, all paid allegiance to the paramount ruler, the *mahārāja*. Beyond the *kraton* the villagers continued to live according to their age-old traditions.

---

[3] According to Lekkerkerker Indian law never usurped Indonesian indigenous *adat*. Although elements of Indian law were included, there was never a complete body of Hindu law in Java. Earlier scholars, according to Lekkerkerker, wrongly interpreted many aspects of law in Indonesia as being Indian. (T.C. Lekkerkerker, *Hindoe-Recht in Indoneië*, 1918, 26, 29).

ADOPTION OF INDIAN PRINCIPLES OF KINGSHIP

Belief in the magico-religious powers of the chieftain existed in Indonesia long before the arrival of Indian influence, and this aura of divinity and magical power which surrounded the chief was essentially the same as that which set the Indian ruler above his fellow men. The Indian concept of kingship included a mystical charisma which gave the ruler superhuman status. Therefore, acceptance by the people of the concept of the divine ruler as a god on earth who would protect them and maintain universal law and harmony in their world, served to strengthen the position of those *rakas* who adopted the cloak of Indian kingship.

According to the concept of ideal kingship the ruler had to measure up to certain standards, both physical and moral. Physical perfection, based on the attribute of the divine Rama, was considered to be a requisite of the ideal king and was a reflection of his inner spiritual strength. He was considered to be an intermediary between his subjects and the divine powers which governed the peace and prosperity of the kingdom. Between the ruler and his people there was thought to exist a mystical bond, which meant that everything which affected the ruler likewise affected his people. If the ruler did not abide by the principles of ideal kingship his subjects suffered as a consequence, and the entire kingdom could be brought to ruin. From a practical viewpoint, in an agrarian kingdom dependent on irrigation this could happen if the ruler neglected his kingly duties.

One of the duties of the ideal ruler was to protect his people and to strive for their welfare. It was the king's responsibility to establish 'good works' such as civic amenities and irrigation and other farming projects. The Old Javanese *Rāmāyaṇa*, through the words of Rama, the paragon of kingly virtues, reminds the rulers that:

> In order to protect the entire kingdom
> You must care for the monasteries, maintain
> holy domains and temples of the gods.
> Roads, resthouses, fountains, lakes, dams
> and fisheries.
>
> Markets, bridges, all that which benefits the people
> you must take care of.[4]
>
> Care of the farmlands is always the king's responsibility
> For from them come all the produce for the kingdom's
> welfare.[5]

In an agrarian kingdom, dependent on an efficient irrigation system, careful control of this system is of paramount importance. If firm and vigilant supervision is lacking the irrigation installation may be rendered ineffective. The channels and conduits would quickly silt up, affecting the productivity of the fields. This would lead to an adverse effect on the economy, which in turn could cause eventual weakness and collapse of the kingdom. Thus, the welfare of the entire region depends on successful productive *sawah* farming which only the control of a higher authority endowed with the necessary resources and manpower can successfully maintain. An example of the successful outcome of intervention of higher authority, when problems arise which the farmers themselves cannot overcome, is found in the Kělagyan inscription. When the farmers along the Brantas valley failed to stem the flooding river, which ruined their *sawah* fields, the ruler Airlangga brought his power and influence to bear.[6]

---

[4]   Chapter 3, stanza 70, translated from Hendrik Kern, *Rāmāyaṇa Kakawin: Oldjavaansch heldendicht*, 1900, hereafter OJR.

[5]   OJR, stanza 78.

[6]   OJO LXI.

In return for his mantle of protection over the realm and for the conscientious performance of his royal duties the king could exercise certain rights and privileges within his realm.

The ruler's rights and privileges

The ruler possessed three basic rights, those of:

1. *drĕwya haji* - the rights to a percentage of the produce from the agricultural regions.[7]

2. *buat haji* or *gawai haji* - the right to employ corvee labour for *kraton* maintenance, temple building, large scale works, etc.

3. *anugraha* - the right to grant favours. For example, the ruler could renounce his *drĕwya haji* entitlement in favour of one of his high-ranking officials or a religious body whom he might wish to reward.[8]

Besides these basic rights the ruler possessed the right, or privilege to 'enjoy' his kingdom, which means that he could live a life of ease and security in his *kraton*, that he was assured of his income from his subjects and as a link with the supernatural forces of nature he held a general though qualified right to land and water within the kingdom.

Drĕwya haji, the 'ruler's due' consisted in the main of a percentage of produce from the farmers' lands. According to ancient *adat*, however, land used for agrarian purposes was never actually the ruler's possession. *Buat haji*, or *gawai haji*, conscription or statute labour, provided the second most important source of royal income. *Buat haji* applied to work done by the villager for the ruler, or service which the ruler was entitled to receive from the villagers;

---

[7] The first known reference to *drĕwya haji* occurs in the Dieng stone of 809 A.D., line 8. (H.B. Sarkar, *Corpus of the Inscriptions of Java*, I, 1972, 50.)

[8] See F.H. van Naerssen, 'Some Aspects of the Hindu-Javanese Kraton', *Journal of the Oriental Society of Australia*, II, 1, 1963, 4.

this included forced labour used to construct the great temples and sanctuaries. Part of *buat haji* consisted of maintenance work within the *kraton* city, also probably providing the transport required for the ruler and his family and large retinue of officials, when on tour through the provinces or *manca nāgara*. Part of *buat haji*, according to some inscriptions, included the making of 'flower baskets' for presentation at funeral sanctuaries of departed rulers at the time of certain festivals. Large-scale irrigation works were provided by the ruler for his subjects, but maintenance and guardianship were carried out by the farmers as *buat haji*, supervised by the ruler's agricultural officers.

Anungraha, the ruler's right to award favours to whomsoever he saw fit is sanctioned by the Old Javanese *Rāmāyaṇa*:

> Those who are diligent and law-abiding
> you should reward with favours,
> For it is the Ruler's prerogative to award
> favours or mete out punishment.[9]

As mentioned in the notes on epigraphy, grants were made by rulers to various subjects and usually consisted of land, gifts of gold or silver, or of precious cloth. Through the system of *anugraha* the ruler could also extend temple building, and public works for the benefit of his subjects, thereby accumulating more merit for himself and fulfilling his kingly duty of 'pleasing' his people and keeping them content at the same time. *Anugraha* was also exercised by princes, or *rakryāns*, to a certain extent.

The ruler's land and water rights

Ownership of agricultural land, including the right to inherit and the right to mortgage, remained within the farmer's jurisdiction,

---

[9] OJR, stanza 75.

the ruler possessing only the right to undeveloped land such as forest land, and probably swampland. The ruler also appears to have 'owned' the neutral land between villages; in Bali the ruler acted as arbitrator between disputing villages and at the same time, by creating a neutral strip of land between them, gained a hold over the area, by 'ownership' of that land.[10] It seems that *rakas* gained agricultural land through marriage to the daughters of landowners, as they appear to have done in later times. The whole question of land and water rights in Java and Bali is very complex, even for present-day conditions. Judgements concerning the ruler's rights in ancient times would be simply guesswork. However, it appears that the ruler possessed only restricted rights, even over domain ground.

There seems to be very little known, and probably very little evidence remains, of the ruler's rights to water in Java. There is reference in the *Nāgarakĕrtāgama* to the purchase of irrigation water 'by the lands of the royal servants'.[11] In Bali it was considered that the ruler had ownership rights to running water, rivers and streams, and this gave him the right to tax his subjects for the water they used on their *sawahs*. The ruler's rights to land therefore depended on the water used to irrigate the land, water which the ruler taxed for a small fee. Interest in his subjects' welfare appears to have justified the ruler's supervision over water supplies for *sawah* use in Bali, and the fact that the ruler was considered to be the 'owner' of the water was because of his

---

[10] See T.C. Lekkerkerker, *Hindoe Recht van Indonesië*, 1918, 31. Lekkerkerker remarks that it seems that in this way the ruler usurped land rights in ancient Java and Bali. See also V.C. Korn, *Het adatrecht van Bali*, 1924, 415.

[11] Pigeaud, III, 147.

identification with the river god. As the ruler in ancient Java also appears to have been identified with the river god the same conditions may have applied. In Java well or spring water was considered to be the property of the owner on whose land the well or spring was located. Liefrinck writes that in Bali ownership of water from wells, besides that from rivers and streams, was 'vested in the ruler' who 'may dispose of it' as he wished.[12]

Taxes and fines

According to Gonggrijp the ruler in ancient Java levied heavy taxes, a fact revealed in Chinese sources of the period 960 to 1279 A.D. For example, Chinese sources of Airlangga's time from 1037 A.D., claim that a tax of one-tenth on rice was levied. A Chinese source of the Sung dynasty of 960-1279 records the levying of one *ch'ien* (one-tenth *tael* or Chinese ounce) of gold for every measured quantity of rice of two and one-fifth *picul* (which is about 3-8 grains of gold from every 135 kilograms), an unbelievably heavy tax according to Gonggrijp.[13] Lekkerkerker writes that the ruler levied a tax of one-sixth of the harvest, and in wartime this was increased to one-quarter.[14]

Pigeaud is also of the opinion that royal taxes placed a heavy burden on the cultivators; and that the royal progress, the tours made by the Majapahit kings, must have depleted the rice supplies and other foods in sparsely populated districts.[15]

---

[12] F.A. Liefrinck, 'Rice Cultivation in Northern Bali', *Bali: Further Studies in Life, Thought, and Ritual*, 1969, 44.

[13] G. Gonggrijp, *Schets eener economische geschiedenis van Indonesie,* 1928, 7. Also W.P. Groeneveldt, *Historical Notes on Indonesia and Malaya. Compiled from Chinese sources*, 1960, 16.

[14] T.C. Lekkerkerker, *Hindoe-Recht van Indonesië*, 1918, 29.

[15] Pigeaud, IV, 304.

In Bali the *tenah winih* is used as a basis for taxation. The same applied in ancient Java (see page 40). Observing by long experience that a given area of *sawah* land of a given level of fertility requires an estimated number of sheaves of rice for seedgrain, taxation officials assessed each sheaf of rice at a fixed amount, payable in kind. Tax levied on rice production payable in cash instead of kind was known in Bali as *tiga sana* and was similar to the water tax, the *suwinih*, in this respect. *Tiga sana*, or cash payment, was explained as tax to the ruler 'who cannot live on rice alone'.[16] Liefrinck observes that *sawah* tax was the most important form of taxation in the early part of this century.[17] In ancient times in Java other forms of taxation, such as festival tax and many others, were also levied but *sawah* tax would have been the major burden.

The cost of measuring or surveying *sawah* fields was recorded in inscriptions. In the Ngabean II copper-plate it states that the total sum of expenses for surveying the *tĕgal* land at Kwak, to convert to *sawah*, was estimated to amount to 1 *sūwarna kā*, 11 *sūwarna*, 5 gold *māsa* and 3 gold *kupang*.[18] Inhabitants of the royal domains were exempt from taxes but instead they were alloted duties towards the sanctuary; for example, they may have been charged to provide a sheep or a certain amount of rice for the yearly sacrifice.[19] In Majapahit

---

[16] R. van Eck and F.A. Liefrinck, 'Kerta sima of Gemeente-en Waterschappen-wetten op Bali', *TBG*, XXIII, 1876, 224.

[17] F.A. Liefrinck, *Landsverordeningen van Inlandsche Vorsten op Bali*, 1917, 313.

[18] H.B. Sarkar, I, 1972, 220, line 14.

[19] See J.G. de Casparis, *Selected Inscriptions from the 7th to the 9th Century A.D.*, 1956, 225, note 59.

times coins were used, while in the ninth, tenth and eleventh centuries, according to the charters, payments were made to the ruler in gold and silver, by weight.

THE STRUCTURE OF THE INDO-JAVANESE KINGDOM

One of the indigenous complexes carried over more or less intact from pre-Indianized times was the concept of communal leadership, the council of *rāmas*, which was adapted to Indo-Javanese conditions. Social rank was based on proximity to the king; the nearer the subject was in relationship, the higher his rank in the hierarchy of the court. The court structure as a whole was based on the pre-Indianized concept of the universe, consisting of concentric circles (which, as noted above, was the indigenous Javanese concept also, applied to the village grouping). The inner circle represented the ruler, as the divine centre, surrounded by the *kraton* as intermediary between the ruler and the outer administration. The second circle represented the *nāgara*, the capital city, seat of the outer administration and residence of princes and other members of the royal family. The third circle was the *nāgara agung*, the greater capital, or the lands outside the city limits held in appanage by princes and nobles, the *rakryāns*. The fourth or outer circle represented the *manca nāgara*, the 'foreign' land, agricultural land in the interior which was administered by headmen appointed by the ruler.

Within the area outside the *kraton* city there were several kinds of agricultural holdings. *Sīma* lands, freehold estates, and domains created by the ruler, and sometimes by *rakryāns* who wished to grant an *anugraha* to loyal officials or priests in their personal service. An early example of the transfer in status of village land to that of a *sīma* holding can be found in a decree issued by King Lokapala in 860

A.D. The king wished to create a *dharmasīma lĕpas*, a freehold domain, for his spiritual mentor the priest of Bodhimimba, who had served him well. By royal command the *dharmasīma lĕpas* was to be marked out and established on land which had been purchased from several village officials of the village Bungur South; land in the village of Kuryyak was also bought for the same purpose. The charter specifically states that the property should be a hereditary freehold, to be inherited by the priest's two children who would then have sole authority over the *dharmasīma*, to be passed on to their descendants forever.[20]

A later inscription, the Suradakan charter of 1447 A.D.,[21] recording the foundation of a freehold *deśa*, district, at Waringin Pitu in East Java gives an indication of the expansion of freehold districts and domains during the period since Lokapala issued his decree in the ninth century. The Waringin Pitu freehold agricultural lands are referred to in the charter as *sang hyang dhārmma*, which Yamin translates as *perdikan-darma* in Bahasa Indonesia.[22] Exact measurements of the area of *sawah* fields and other agricultural land to be included in the *perdikan-darma* are given.

Sīma land was exempt from *drĕwya haji* and *gawai haji*. The ruler's tax collectors, the *mangilala drĕwya haji*, were forbidden to enter the *sīma* estates. Being free from royal taxes the *sīma* estates used the surplus from the land for their own purposes. Apart from freehold domains and estates, villages were also given *sīma* status; in return

---

[20] Kancaña copper-plates, Pl.1, B:6 to Pl. V, A:3 (Sarkar, I, 134-37).

[21] Muhammid Yamin, *Petulisan Widjaja-Parakrama-Wardana dari Surodakan (Kediri) dengan bertarich sjaka 1368-T.M. 1447*, 1962. See also B.J.O. Shrieke, 'Iets over Perdikan-instituut', *TBG*, LVIII, 1919, 391-425.

[22] Yamin, 26.

for the privileges that accompanied *sīma* status the villagers were obliged to apply themselves to a certain project. For example, the villagers of Kamalagyan were required to settle by the *sīma* dam built by Airlangga at Waringin Sapta, in order to 'take care' of the dam, to guard against damage or destruction.[23] Most *sīmas* appear to have been created in favour of religious communities; they were probably awarded by the ruler with a view to gaining merit or enhancing his position as a just and magnanimous ruler.

In the *nāgara agung*, the *rakryāns*, princes, and other nobles held administrative provinces, *watěks* (sometimes *watak*), over which they held authority but which were under the jurisdiction of the ruler. The *rakryāns* held rights to the produce from the land, but unlike *sīma* land, *watěks* were subject to *drěwya haji*. Clustered within these regions, which the Dutch writers referred to as appanges, were villages over which the *watěk* held jurisdiction. In Śrī Kahulunan's inscription of 842 A.D. the phrase *wanwa i tru i tpussan watak= kahulunan* ... appears, which reads 'the village of Teru i Tepusan under (the jurisdiction of) the Queen Kahulunan ...'.[24] The earliest reference to *watěks* is found in the Dieng stone of 809 A.D. wherein it states that, *hana sīma i panulingan watak [watěk] pikatan sawah ...* 'there is a freehold at Panulingan under Pikatan of *sawah* fields'.[25]

---

[23] OJO LXI, Kělagyan inscription of 1037 A.D., lines 15-16.

[24] J.G. de Casparis, *Inscripties uit de Çailendra-tijd*, 1950, 86, 91 (inscription of Śrī Kahulunan, II, line 2).

[25] Sarkar, I, 50 (verso, lines 2-3).

The rakryāns

The title of *rakryān*[26] was usually applied to princes who ranked next to the king at court, probably his younger brothers. *Rakas* and *rakryāns* seem to have held much the same degree of rank and some are referred to as both *raka* and *rakryān* in the same inscription. Both held positions of the highest authority in ancient Javanese *kraton* society, such as *mahāmantri*, chief minister, and a ruler could rise from the ranks of either the *rakas* or the *rakryāns*. Apart from their duties within the general administration of the kingdom, the *rakryāns* exercised authority over their own principalities or appanages. However, Stutterheim points out that they did not hold such an extensive authority over their agricultural lands as the village administration or the villagers themselves held over their land. Rather, in Stutterheim's opinion, the *rakryāns* and the *rakas* stood in a magical relationship with the ground, connected with their choice of what was to be their burial ground. Their names were mostly identified with stones of various shapes or forms, or trees of various kinds. In this respect, Stutterheim notes the

---

[26] Sarkar suggests that the term *raka* may have been an abbreviation of *rakryān* which he derives from the Sanskrit *karya* or *kriya* with the Indonesian honorific prefix *ra* and the suffix *an*. (H.B. Sarkar, 'Survey of Some Aspects of Old-Javanese Inscriptions of Central Java' in Buddha Prakash (ed.), *Studies in Asian History and Culture*, 1970, 48. Van Naerssen maintains that the word *raka* is an ancient Indonesian word meaning elder brother in its original sense. (F.H. van Naerssen, 'Some Aspects of the Hindu-Javanese Kraton', *Journal of the Oriental Society of Australia*, II, 1, 1963, 17.) Goris notes that the title *rakryān* appeared in Balinese inscriptions for the first time during the reign of Udayana, Airlangga's father. (Roelof Goris, *Prasasti Bali*, II, 295.) The usually accepted explanation for *rakryān* is that it derives from *ra-kriyān* (Balinese, *klyan*, modern *klian*).

similarity between the *rakryāns* of Java and the *karaengs* of Makassar, who also held an 'ornament' or symbolic rank of a magical nature, who, as in Java, also could rise to the rank of ruler of a kingdom, and whose power was connected with magical objects such as stones, and other things of an animistic nature.[27]

The *rakryāns* and *rakas* maintained contact with the land through the *mangilala drĕwya haji*, a group of people who appear to have performed special functions in court society, perhaps with some magical overtones.[28] Both the ruler and the *rakryāns* employed *mangilala drĕwya haji*,[29] to collect the taxes and dues. *Rakryāns* were entitled to receive *drĕwya haji* and *gawai* or *buat haji* from their own subjects, and they had their own officials and servants on their appanages to attend to agrarian matters, the most prominent among whom were the *nāyakas* (nowadays *bekels*). In a copper-plate of unknown origin dating from 924 A.D. the *rakryāns*' 'servants' are specifically mentioned. The inscription contains a long list (although by no means the longest in inscriptions) of officials and servants who were forbidden to enter freehold grounds.[30] *Rakryāns* apparently had authority to grant *anugraha* to favoured subjects; in the copper-plates of Panggumulan it is recorded that the *rakryān* of Wantil pu (mpu) Palaka, his wife *dyah* (princess) Prasada and his three sons gave land to 'the god and goddess of Kinawuhan'.[31] *Rakryāns* apparently wielded

---

[27] W.F. Stutterheim, 'Iets over raka en rakryan naar aanleiding van Sindok's dynastieke positie', *TBG*, LXXIII, 1933, 167.

[28] Stutterheim, 166.

[29] See de Casparis, II, 240, note 171.

[30] Sarkar, II, 209-10, lines 9-16.

[31] Sarkar, II, 31, lines 2-4.

considerable authority in ancient Java. The three Chief Ministers, the *mahāmantris* of Hino, Sirikan and Halu, the highest officials in the kingdom, were always *rakryāns* or *rakas*.

Samĕgats (pamĕgats)

Apparently *samĕgats* were also of noble birth[32] and bore a rank of considerable importance within the structure of *kraton* administration, although Pigeaud translates the term, in the context of fourteenth century Majapahit, as 'a gentleman'. From Balitung's reign to at least Siṇḍok's time the title seems to have ranked just under that of *raka* and *rakryān*. In the lists of those high dignitaries to receive ceremonial gifts at foundation ceremonies the *samĕgats* are generally listed with the *rakryāns*. In Balitung's charter of 907 A.D. this is found to be the case. In the same charter there is a reference to the Samĕgat of Kalangwungkul who was accompanied by his four wives, each of whom bore the rank of *samĕgat*, whether because of their husband's title or as their own right is not known.[33] The priest who conducted the ceremony, administered the oaths and so on, was also entitled Pamĕgat Makudur. Some *samĕgats* bore the honorific *sang* before their title and probably belonged to the priestly class. In the Bakalan inscription the two *samĕgats* mentioned appear to be the only court officials involved in the execution of Rakryān Mangibil's decree, besides *mpunta* (Reverend) Pakatuppan and possibly the *patih* mentioned in the list of those receiving ceremonial gifts.

---

[32] In Malay the title *megat* occurs as a princely title, for example, Megat of Trengganu.

[33] See F.H. van Naerssen, 'Twee Koperen Oorkonden van Balitung in het Koloniaal Instituut te Amsterdam Holland', *BKI*, XCV, 1937, 455.

Other court officials

Long lists of officials appear in inscriptions, following after the *rakryāns* and *samĕgats*.[34] Further down the ranks of court hierarchy were the officials classified as *wadwa* who apparently were entitled to use the honorific *sang*. The *wadwa* in turn had their own representatives, the *pawuwus* or *parujar*, who probably acted as proxy for the *wadwas* at foundation ceremonies and other matters in outlying agrarian regions.[35] The persons heading the lower group of court dignitaries, who always appear first on the lists of those officials forbidden to trespass on freehold farmland, were the *pangkur*, *tawan* and *tirup*. These three officials possessed the authority to collect the royal taxes, and they retained their position of importance throughout the Indo-Javanese period.[36] They are first mentioned in charters as early as the Kalasan inscription of 778 A.D. At that time they seem to have held positions of a religious nature.

Javanese rulers could only exert their influence over a comparatively limited area in ancient times due to natural geographical fragmentation, and to primitive means of communication. Therefore certain court officials were delegated to oversee the

---

[34] It is apparent from the Perot inscription of 850 A.D., for example, that Rakryān Patapan had a very large number of personnel at his disposal. See the two inscriptions from Candi Perot (de Casparis, II, 211-43). De Casparis (p.220) points out that this inscription is the earliest known example containing a regular list of court dignitaries following reference to the king.

[35] See de Casparis, II, 224.

[36] See Sarkar, I, 39, note 39 and De Casparis, II, 221, note 48 concerning *wadwa*. Van Naerssen considers them to have been notable village heads. (F.H. van Naerssen, 'The Çailendra Interregnum' *India Antiqua*, 1947, 250).

outlying agrarian regions, to guard the king's interests. In many inscriptions long lists of court functionaries are given, but the meaning of most of these titles remain unknown or are subject to guesswork.

WOMEN IN OLD JAVANESE AGRARIAN SOCIETY

Takdir Alisjahbana, writing of the special place women hold in Indonesian society, remarks that:

> It is not surprising .... that there are sociologists and historians who believe that women were the first agriculturists and regular workers, and that it was women who patiently and systematically sowed the crops and worked at the handicrafts .... It was the matriarchal society which typically was the first to settle down permanently in a fixed area and gain its livelihood from regular agricultural and craft pursuits.[37]

From many references in Old Javanese inscriptions it is clear that women held a comparatively high place in ancient Javanese society, either in various official capacities or as respected wives of both village and court officials. However, the women mentioned in old charters were of royal birth or were high dignitaries in rural society. There are records of women having held the exalted rank of *mahārāja* and of *raka* while others bore the titles of *rakryāns*, *samĕgats* and *rāmas*.[38] There is no direct evidence of the position held by women in other classes of Old Javanese society. De Casparis considers

---

[37] Takdir Alisjahbana, *Indonesia: Social and Cultural Revolution*, 1951, 105.

[38] See H.B. Sarkar, *Corpus of the Inscriptions of Java*, II, 95 and 225; F.H. van Naerssen, 'Twee Koperen Oorkonden van Balitung in het Koloniaal Instituut te Amsterdam Holland', *BKI*, XCV, 1937, 455.

that women from the ranks of commoners probably possessed the same rights and privileges as those from the higher ranks but that they may not have exercised their rights.[39]

The number of inscriptions issued by queens ruling in ancient Java is very small. However, the few available reveal the fact that not only the principal consort of certain rulers but secondary queens also, were ruling independently over their own territory, with the authority to dispose of land for the purpose of establishing freehold *sawah* lands. The earliest reference to a ruling queen in Java is found in Chinese records of the New Tang Dynasty which report that in 674 A.D. the kingdom of Ho-ling was ruled so well by Queen Sīma that 'a bag of gold could be left by the side of the road and no one would attempt to steal it'.[40]

The earliest inscription, and the only one from Central Java issued by a woman belongs to the Raka of Pikatan's consort, Śri Kahulunan. Issued in 842 A.D.[41] it records the donation of a certain number of *sawah* fields towards the upkeep of a funerary temple built for her late father, Samaratungga, the last Śailendra ruler. Śri Kahulunan appears to have been a woman of some considerable standing. She was probably one of several lesser independent rulers in Central Java at the end of the Śailendra period. From East Java comes a

---

[39] J.G. de Casparis, *Inscripties uit de Çailendra-tijd*, 1950, 107.

[40] W.P. Groeneveldt, *Historical Notes on Indonesia and Malaya from Chinese Historical Sources*, 1960, 14.

[41] De Casparis, 86-7. De Casparis (107 and note 7) draws attention to Stutterheim's theories concerning the connection between women and groundrights in ancient Java; as women may not have used these rights, de Casparis considers that Śri Kahulunan's land transaction in 842 A.D. must have been of great significance.

similar inscription nearly a century later issued in King Siṇḍok's time by Rakryān Binihaji Parameśwarī Dyah Kĕbi, recording the founding of a funerary sanctuary for her father and the granting of *sawah* lands made freehold for the upkeep of the sanctuary.[42]

Another East Javanese queen to record the granting of freehold rights to irrigated farmland, as well as hunting grounds, for the upkeep of a religious foundation, was the mysterious Mahārāja Nari, also called Paduka Śri Mahādewi in the same charter.[43] The latter title, according to van Naerssen, suggests that she was a secondary queen of an unnamed ruler, although she was herself ruling in Keḍiri, a fact stated in the inscription. As her decree was issued in 1015 A.D., only eight years before King Airlangga's earliest inscription, van Naerssen asks if she may have been Airlangga's mother or wife or daughter.[44]

A further record of land disposal by a woman ruler is found in the Karang Bogĕm charter of 1387 A.D.,[45] issued jointly by the Princess of Lasĕm, daughter of the Majapahit ruler Hayam Wuruk, and her consort the Prince of Mataram. The ground released by order of the Princess for the newly created state of Karang Bogĕm, was to be used for terraced *sawah* cultivation. This land measured seven acres, one *jung*. A further three and a half acres, one *kikil*, of cleared land was to

---

[42] See W.F. Stutterheim, 'Epigraphica', *TBG*, LXXV, 1935, 456-61; N.J. Krom, *Hindoe-Javaansche qeschiedenis*, 1931, 213.

[43] F.H. Naerssen, *Oudjavaansche Oorkonden in Duitsche en Deensche Verzamelingen*, 1941, (Inscription VII: 1A, line 4 and VII:2B, lines 3-4).

[44] Van Naerssen, 80.

[45] Th. Pigeaud, *Java in the 14th Century*, 1960-3, II, 452 and IV, 449.

be set aside for the use of a Gresik fisherman and his family; this man was appointed by the Princess as steward in charge of the royal fisheries.[46]

There is ample evidence that women owned land in their own right in ancient Java. An inscription which throws some light on this aspect of women's rights to ownership, and disposal, of agricultural land is the Kinawĕ charter of 927 A.D.[47] issued by a woman ruler, the Raka of Gunungan, East Java. The inscription records that the *raka*, *dyah* Muatan '... the mother of Bingah, marked out the village at Kinawĕ under Kadangan. Now, the reason is that the marked-out free-hold shall be inherited by her grand-children through her (own) son, but shall not accrue to the half-brothers and sisters of *dyah* Bingah from the father's side (?). Because, this free-hold is not the free-hold of the *rakryān*, her husband.'[48] The inscription indicates the sole rights the *raka* exercised over her own property, over which her husband had no control. There is indirect evidence of women's land rights in the Taji inscription of 901 A.D.[49] Among the names of the owners of land purchased by the Rakryān of Watu for the purpose of setting out *sawah* fields and garden land for the upkeep of the temple of Desawambha, were the names of two women, *si* Padas and *si* Mendut, the mothers of Sumag and Mangas.[50]

---

[46] Pigeaud, IV, 450.

[47] Sarkar, II, 224-6.

[48] Sarkar, 225, lines 7-9. Sarkar draws attention to *dyah* Muatan's rank (note 20), which was above that of her husband who was a *rakryān*. (Although the distinction between the titles is apparently slight.)

[49] Sarkar, 8.

[50] Women were identified as 'the mother of --' in inscriptions where they are referred to specifically.

Women were also represented in the legal field in ancient Java. The copper-plate inscription, a *jayapattra* of 907 A.D.,[51] concerns a law suit over a debt previously incurred by *si* Campa, the deceased wife of *pu* Tabwel of Guntur. A relative of the dead woman, to whom the gold was owed, had the widower brought to judgement before six persons, the *saměgat* Pinapan, the *saměgat*'s wife and four witnesses. Because *pu* Tabwel had been unaware of his wife's debt, and because she had died childless (besides the fact that the claimant failed to appear at court) the case was dismissed. The relevance of the case here is the fact that wives were apparently able to conduct their own affairs independently of their husbands, even to the extent of incurring debts. The husband on the other hand was not answerable for his wife's debt if he had been unaware of it, and if he was without an heir. Furthermore, the fact that a woman, the *saměgat* Pinapan's wife, sat in judgement at the trial is an indication of women's access to positions of authority in ancient Java.

Besides records of women actually owning and disposing of land there is evidence that women took an active part in ceremonies connected with the granting of land for freehold domains. Wives of the village heads, elders and other officials from neighbouring villages who were attending the ceremony also took their appointed place . According to the Amsterdam II inscription wives sat facing the priestly officials, *sang wahuta hyang kudur*, and the sacred foundation stone placed in the centre of the official gathering.[52] The women received ceremonial gifts according to their rank and in

---

[51] Sarkar, 99-101.

[52] Van Naerssen, 'Twee Oorkonden', 456.

accordance with the importance of the freehold grant. Gifts usually consisted of either cloth (*kain*) for ceremonial wear, or cloth and a measure of gold or silver. The Taji inscription[53] records that in a large foundation ceremony attended by 392 officials the wives received *kain* and two measures of gold each, however, one woman, apparently of more importance than others, received a special length of 'eastern' cloth (*buatan wĕtan*) and a gold ring weighing eight *māsa*.[54] In the Kĕmbang Arum charter mothers and their children are listed, each woman and child by name, as recipients of gifts of cloth and silver. Older women and wives of young men are listed in separate categories.[55]

THE BOND BETWEEN THE KRATON AND THE WANUA

As far as agrarian development in ancient Java was concerned the pattern of kingship was the most significant element of Indian culture to be superimposed on the Indonesian way of life. The villages, which until the principles of Indian kingship were introduced and a more elaborate and enlarged centre of authority established, had need to produce only sufficient for their own consumption now had to produce enough to contribute to the king and his court, and to the army. The villagers filled a dual role, that of suppliers of rice for the *kraton* within their district, to be used for both consumption and export, and as a source of manpower for the construction and maintenance of temples and *kraton* buildings.

Sawah cultivation on an intensive scale demands a high degree of co-operation not only between villages but between the village and the

---

[53] Sarkar, II, 10.

[54] Th. Pigeaud, 'Javanese Gold', *BKI*, LXIV, 1958, 194.

[55] Sarkar, II, 34-5.

central administration, the court. Economic growth and prosperity depend on a stable organization at both levels. During the whole of the Indo-Javanese period there appear to have been two distinct forms of government, one purely indigenous at village level, and the other an Indianized form of administration at *kraton* level. Van Naerssen writes that:

> ... before the coming of Indian influence Javanese society consisted of a large number of small exclusive *adat* societies who each had their own history, *adat* and customs, their own government and administration. Then a royal government was introduced, but the ruler of this administration saw to it that the various social groups, or village settlements under his jurisdiction remained undisturbed as far as possible, to follow their own pattern of life. Because of this, during practically the entire period of Indo-Javanese history there were two forms of government existing side by side, the village government and the court government as a 'mantle of protection' over the various villages under its care. The first was represented by the *rāmas* and the second by the Indianized *raka* and his staff of high ranking officials.[56]

The *kraton* and the *wanua* depended on each other in a situation of expanding agrarian economy. The village was dependent on the ruler for public works such as bridges, roads, irrigation projects and other amenities, and for protection from possible threat; the *kraton* was dependent on the village for food supplies, manpower for military service and for *buat haji*, corvee labour. Irrigation works on a large scale were established by order of the ruler; the rural population lacked the facilities for such projects. The success of a hydraulic kingdom, however, could only be achieved and maintained by a communal effort on the part of both the *kraton* and the village.

---

56 Van Naerssen, 'Twee Koperen Oorkonden van Balitung', 447. See also F.H. van Naerssen and R.C. de Iongh, *The Economic and Administrative History of Early Indonesia*, Leiden, 1977.

The people of the rural areas looked to the *kraton* for protection and assistance. They saw the *kraton* city as a reflection of the universe wherein the gods maintained the balance of harmony and prosperity, where the *raka*, the divine ruler filled the role of protector and preserver of harmony and prosperity within this universe on earth. According to the principles of ideal kingship the ruler was pledged to abide by the codes of conduct and kingly precepts, to protect and care for his subjects. In return he received their loyalty and service. Rama said:

> You the King are like a great mountain and your
> subjects are the trees upon it.
> It is the balance of harmony between the highest
> and the lowest that maintains prosperity and happiness.[57]

---

[57] OJR, stanza 77.

CHAPTER FOUR

RELIGIOUS ASPECTS OF AGRARIAN LIFE
IN ANCIENT JAVA

In no study concerning agrarian life in Indonesia can the religious aspect be omitted, for we are, as Zoetmulder points out, 'observing a culture which has to a high degree been formed by religion'.[1] In Java, and in fact everywhere in Indonesia, there exists an inherent belief in spirits, both divine and malevolent; there is also a belief in the power of various spirits to protect or to punish those who earn their blessing or displeasure. A vast system of ritual and taboo govern the life of the agricultural community and every farmer enveavours to control the vengeance of evil spirits who might bring disease and misfortune to his household, animals and crops.

Belief in *semangat*, the vital force which is thought to inhabit things both animate and inanimate, is widespread among rural folk, especially those from the more isolated regions. This vital force is considered to dwell in soil, plants, rocks, rivers, trees and mountains as well as in man himself. Winstedt wrote of early man's animistic search for identity thus:

> Casting about for an image of the personal soul, the Malay noted the flutter of the heart, the vital spark in the fire-fly, the stridulous telegraphy of the cricket in the camphor-tree, the uncanny likeness of the stick-insect to the rattan. So he found the soul of a camphor-tree in the cicada, the

---

[1] P.J. Zoetmulder, 'The Significance of the Study of Culture and Religion for Indonesian Historiography', in Soedjatmoko, (ed.). *An Introduction to Indonesian Historiography*, 1965, 327.

> soul of rice in the grass-hopper, the soul
> of the rattan in the stick-insect, the souls
> of man and the coconut-palm in a bird.[2]

Living as they do close to nature, the inhabitants of the villages of Java have retained many of their animistic beliefs. Each village possesses its own particular rural spirits, guardians of the soil, of water and of crops. Hamlets attached to villages worship the spirits of the mother village, the *ḍang hyang desa*; only freehold hamlets possess their own agricultural guardian spirits.[3]

An important aspect of the Indonesian's world view in ancient times was the concept of harmony between the two worlds, heaven and earth, based on the belief that his world is but a reflection of the cosmic world beyond. Belief in the inseparability of heaven and earth found expression in all aspects of his daily life and his aim was continually directed towards maintaining harmony between his own small world and that of the gods. This world view, particularly among the rural communities, persists to the present. As Moertono expresses it:

> The activities of man within and thus towards
> this society in which he lives are mainly
> directed to maintaining this harmony within
> his sphere of life. He must take preventative
> and repressive measures against all possible
> disturbances of his social order and, because
> of the assumed mutual dependency between the
> micro- and the macro-cosmos, of the universal
> order also. In this sense social organization
> is not involvement in the members' daily
> routine but in maintaining adherence to

---

[2] Richard Winstedt, *The Malays. A Cultural History*, 1961, 20.

[3] See J.H.F. Sollewijn Gelpke, 'Het desabestuur op Java. Een bijdrage tot de kennis van Land en Volk', *De Indische Gids*, I, 2, 1879, 136.

> established social patterns, the main manifestation
> of harmony .... In agrarian countries where man's
> life depends so much more on the steady flow of
> seasonal change, where the concept of harmony is
> viewed more in terms of regularity and familiarity
> with the pattern of community life, any interference
> in the life of society may disturb the balance of the
> universe.[4]

RICE GROWING CEREMONIES

For the rice farmer and his family every phase of rice cultivation has a religious significance and special rituals apply to each stage of the rice plant's life. These rituals are a blend of indigenous animistic beliefs and Hinduism, with later additions from Islamic influence. Van Akkeren, writing of rites considered necessary for the successful cultivation of rice, notes that:

> ... these must create the highest possible
> level of harmony and solidarity between the
> mood of the spirits and the frame of mind of
> the farmers. The powers of heaven and earth,
> especially those of the chthonic side of the
> cosmos, must be coaxed into a mood of extreme
> good will.[5]

Everywhere in the *sawah* regions of Indonesia the rice plant is considered as a living person, requiring attention and care from birth to death. The development of rice, from the seedling to the grain ripe for harvesting, is likened to the physical process of human growth and the plants are treated accordingly. The life of the rice is believed to be constantly dependent upon the guardianship of spiritual forces and, providing the necessary ritual is observed, the

---

[4] Soemarsaid Moertono, *State and Statecraft in Old Java*, 1968, 3-4.

[5] Philip van Akkeren, *Sri and Christ*, 1970, 167.

rice is protected by the deities, the foremost of which is Śri the rice goddess. Dewi Śri is looked upon as the embodiment of all *semangat*, the life force which generates, nourishes and watches over each and every rice plant. Śri represents the whole field of rice; as van Akkeren expresses it '... it is she who keeps the rice from the whole field together during the terrible period (terrible for the rice which is seen as a person) when the rice is cut, pounded, cooked etc ...' and furthermore, '... as a concentration of the spirit of the rice, Śri calls her rice-folk together and lures the lost rice-souls towards her'.[6]

The name Śri is said to have been borrowed from an Indian goddess, Visnu's consort, although Quaritch Wales does not agree on this point. He considers that Śri is to be identified with the Bengal rice goddess Devi.[7] Śri and her partner Sedana, identified with Sardhana, another name for Visnu, are the divine couple linked with the remote ancestors of the Javanese and Balinese people. Grader draws attention to the apparent relationship between the worship of ancestors and the worship of Śri and Sadana (Sedana) in Bali.[8] In Java and Bali the couple are associated with the fertility of both man and rice.

The fertilizing of the rice plants is considered to be brought about by contact of the grain with water, flowing either from irrigation channels or descending from the mountainside to the rice field. The union takes place within the sacred earth when Śri, as

---

[6] Van Akkeren, 18 and 20.

[7] H.G. Quaritch Wales, *The Making of Greater India*, 1961, 111.

[8] C.J. Grader, 'The State Temples of Měngwi', *Bali: Studies in Life, Thought, and Ritual*, 1960, 168-9.

the rice seed, meets Visnu, the water. Śri here represents the concept of death, rebirth and growth. She becomes incarnate in the rice by the process of dying, and as the seed grain she is buried in the earth. There she meets with Visnu, himself reborn in the water, and their marriage takes place, the joining of the rice seed and the water, the ovum and the semen. Thus begins the life cycle leading ultimately to the yellowing grain, after which it enters the earth again and the never-ending cycle continues.[9]

Śri, under her Indian guise, is the primeval Earth Mother. In this guise she is the Goddess of Death, from whom springs all life anew, for man, animals and plants. Can Śri the Rice Goddess be identified with Durga, who is also the Goddess of Death? Krom has recorded the large number of Durga statues found in Java, and also many which appear to represent Śri, and unidentified female figures which may represent either goddess or both.[10] A thorough investigation into the Durga-Śri relationship may bring to light some interesting conclusions. In Bali Śri has four other manifestations, Uma, Durga, Giriputri and Ibu Pertiwi, depending on when she makes her appearance. As Śri herself, she is the goddess of the growing rice plants and the ripening ears of grain. As Uma, she is the deity of both *sawah* and *tegalan*, bringing to life the seed within the earth. She is Durga in her aspect of the goddess of the temple of the dead, supervising the demons who bring diseases and plagues of pests to the growing crops. Giriputri is her

---

[9] See R.M. Sutjipto Wirjosuparto, *Apa sebabnya Kediri dan daerah sekitarnya tampil kemuka dalam sedjarah*, 1958, 112-13 for his remarks on C.C. Berg's views on agricultural symbolism in the Calon Arang.

[10] N.J. Krom, *Inleiding tot de Hindoe-Javaansche Kunst*, II, 295-410.

manifestation as goddess of the sacred mountain Gunung Agung, consort of the mountain god Mahadewa. Pilgrimages are made to Gunung Agung by the rural folk who come to ask of these two deities holy water from their sacred slopes, water to sprinkle on the *sawah* fields and in the irrigation channels. When the deity of the soil, the Earth Mother herself is venerated, Ibu Pertiwi is her name.[11]

Kruyt remarks on the similarity of customs and beliefs concerning rice cultivation in all parts of Indonesia where rice is grown, and especially in regions untouched by Indian influence.[12] Van Eerde, writing of ancient customs and beliefs among the Sasaks of Lombok, describes planting and harvesting rituals observed by the rice farmers.[13] When the rice seedlings are ready for transplanting the owner of the field first selects nine seedlings and plants them near the irrigation inlet to the field, the most important part of the field. Each seedling must consist of a certain number of stalks, ranging from one to nine, and must be planted in a fixed order. One plant is placed in the centre with the remaining eight around it, representing the eight points of the compass plus the centre. Later, from this plot of specially selected and carefully tended rice plants the ripened ears will be harvested to become the 'bridal pair', the *inan pare* or *nini pantun*. The significance of this ritual planting of the first nine seedlings is

---

[11] See Grader, 166-7.

[12] A.C. Kruyt, 'Gebruiken bij de rijstoogst in enkele streken op Oost-Java', *MNZG*, XLVII, 1903, 47. See Parsudi Suparlan, 'Upatjara panenan padi', *Manusia Indonesia*, nomor 1-6, 1969, 49-52 for present-day rice harvest ceremonies.

[13] J.C. van Eerde, 'Gebruiken bij den Rijstbouw en Rijstoogst in Lombok', *TBG*, XLV, 1902, 563-74.

long forgotten; the farmers have no explanation for it other than that it is an ancient custom which they never fail to observe.

When the rice ears begin to swell they are treated as pregnant women. Rice pap or eggs are placed by the irrigation inlet and *daun lego-lego*, or *legundi*, are burnt there to ward off evil spirits. This is seen as the 'drying out' period, the *pendedeng*, which is likened to the several days when a woman, after giving birth, is placed close to a fire kept continually stoked. The rice plants are also offered sour fruits to appease their craving, as a pregnant woman may crave sour food. Sometimes water is sprinkled over the 'pregnant' plants after the water has either had cooling mendicaments added or has stood for a time in a sacred place, such as an ancient grave or seat of the gods. This is to ensure a full harvest. Van Eerde notes that the Baduis of Java have the same customs concerning 'pregnant' rice.[14]

When the rice is ripe, before harvesting commences, the farmer cuts the ears from the nine plants and from these two bundles are made, each consisting of 108 stalks with the leaves left on, to represent the *inan pare*, the divine pair. One bundle is bound with white cord until the leaves are no longer visible; this represents the bridegroom. The 'female' bundle is bound so that the leaves form the shape of a woman's hairknot. The two bundles are then bound together and placed near the irrigation inlet, to remain there whilst the rest of the rice crop is harvested. During harvest the reapers may not make any undue noise, as this might disturb or upset the rice goddess Śri who has descended and entered the grain.

---

[14] Van Eerde, 556, note 1.

The harvesting must be executed with care so that no grains fall to the ground, otherwise the rice goddess in these lost grains will grieve for her sister grains, from whom she will be parted forever when the harvest is taken to the rice barn. While the reaping is in progress the severed ears with a part of the stalk attached are placed on the ground, never on the *sawah* dikes. If this precaution is not observed it is believed that mice will attack the rice when it is stored in the barn. Likewise, the pole used to carry the rice away from the field is never placed on the dike, for fear that evil spirits will later devour the rice in the barn. If the harvest is not completed by evening the leaves on the remaining plants are looped over so that malevolent spirits cannot commence harvesting the rice for themselves during the night.

When the harvested rice is taken from the fields to the rice barn the *nini pantun*, or the *inan pare*, is carefully carried by a woman who guards it against any upset during transit. The Sasak custom is to lay the *nini pantun* on a cushion of rice straw placed on the floor of the rice barn. In some regions of Lombok the 'bridal pair' rests on half a coconut shell in which are nine *kemiri* nuts and nine small black stones. *Mantras* are recited at this time; in fact, *mantras* against plague and pest are recited at all significant phases of rice growing; at seed planting time and again when the owner of the field transplants the *bibit* to the *inan pare* plot, Śri is called upon. Śri is again invoked when the young plants develop new leaves and when the swollen ears of grain are finally cut. Some *mantras* are in Sasak or Balinese but, according to van Eerde, most *mantras* are uttered in Old Javanese.[15]

---

[15] Van Eerde, 574.

In his article concerning customs and ritual observed during the rice harvest in parts of East Java, Kruyt gives the following details. When the rice begins to yellow the farmer seeks a *dukun*, either man or woman, who chooses an auspicious day on which to commence harvest. Tuesday-*Kliwon* is considered a day most suited to Dewi Śri for her descent to the rice field. The *dukuns*, Kruyt remarks, have a saying:

> *Paing* is a good day to begin work in the field.
> *Pon* is a suitable day to sow the rice seed.
> *Wage* is the best day to plant out the rice seedlings.
> *Kliwon* is an auspicious day to begin harvesting.
> *Legi* is the best day to take home the *padi*.

When the day has been fixed the *dukun* rises very early, goes to the *sawah* and plants in each of the four corners of the field a bamboo cylinder containing *badeg*, a liquid made from fermented black rice and *janur*, young palm leaves or coconut tops. This is called '*belabar janur kuning*' and a sign that from now on no one may enter the field. The *dukun* must remain awake during the night before he performs the harvest ritual; sometimes the farmer arranges a *wayang* performance of the Śri and Sedana myth to help him keep awake. At daybreak a *slametan* is held when special dishes are provided, one for Śri and one for the god of vegetation.

Around 7 a.m. the *dukun* goes to the field accompanied by neighbouring farmers, each carrying offerings to leave in the field for Dewi Śri. The *dukun* chooses a place in the centre of the field and proceeds to burn incense. He turns his face to the house of the *sawah* owner and recites 'I feed you with fragrant rice. I call you, Mbok Śri, to your dwelling place here. May you give strength and prosperity' and similar speeches. The *dukun* then commences to cut the rice, as many ears as the total numerical value of the day chosen for the commencement of harvesting, eleven if it happened to be Tuesday-*Kliwon* (the numbers three - Tuesday - and eight - *Kliwon* - totalling eleven). The bundle of ears is tied together, interlaced with flowers and smeared with a fragrant ungent, *kembang boreh*, and placed on a new mat. When taken home, it is placed on a pillow and covered with a fine cloth until the time comes for it to be dried and carefully preserved. After taking the bundle, the *nini* or Rice Mother home, the farmer returns to his field and cuts sufficient rice for one sheaf. Whilst doing this he must not speak or be spoken to. The sheaf is taken home immediately, dried, pounded and cooked as a *sega-polong*, rice-ball, to be used with other dishes in a *slametan sedekah bumi*, to pay homage to the earth and water, without which the rice could not grow. The field is then open to everyone to help with the harvest.

Kruyt remarks that no religious significance is attached to the harvested rice during the period when the sheaves are being distributed among the harvesters as payment, and the balance, the *sawah* owner's sheaves, is taken home. The day the rice harvest is taken to the barn must be an auspicious day, usually a Friday-*Legi*, and a *dukun* is on hand to consecrate the rice barn as the sheaves are stacked inside. The 'bridal pair' have been made and placed on the rice sheaves. The *dukun* then invokes Śri and Sedana. 'Mbok Sri', he calls, 'I have brought you home. I have prepared your home for you in the *gedong si lara Ḍenok*. Sleep well in this very pleasant place Mbok Śri and Sedana. You are now with *jaka tani* (the owner). Allow *jaka tani* to live a life free of all worry and care. May Mbok Śri's fortune continue to flow out from this very pleasant place'.[16]

---

[16] The above translations are from Kruyt, 125-39.

When all the rice is in the barn the *dukun* utters further incantations to Śri, Uma and Kali, and threatens any lurking evil spirits who may disturb the slumbering Śri. The *dukun* then walks around the rice sheaves three times, carrying a bottle of consecrated water. On the fortieth day after harvest a *slametan* is held and dishes are offered to Dewi Śri and other deities. Not until after this day may the rice be used. Several sheaves from the harvest are held out to tide the family over this period.

Geertz writes that nowadays crop *slametans* are still held but only for *sawah*, not for dry-rice crops. As in Kruyt's time, and probably for untold generations earlier, the farmer enlists a *dukun* to work out the most auspicious day on which to commence tilling the soil. A small *slametan* called *wiwit sawah* is held in the field during midmorning, to celebrate 'beginning the rice field' and another is held in the farmer's home. At the time of sowing the rice seed in the *pesemaian*, the seedbed, and again before transplanting the *bibit* to the *sawah* fields *slametans* may be held, although Geertz notes that these are often omitted today. Towards the end of the growing period, and again after the first weeding, when the rice plants begin to bend with the weight of the grain a 'rice pregnancy' *slametan* is held in the owner's home.[17]

The most important crop ceremony, Geertz reports, is the *slametan metik* held to celebrate the harvest and still carried out on a fairly elaborate scale, especially in the villages. The harvest ritual enacts the marriage of Batara Guru's daughter Tisnawati to a mortal, Jakasudana. The Tisnawati and the Śri myths have here become syncretized. About one month before the crop is ripe for

---

[17] C. Geertz, *The Religion of Java*, 1964, 80-81.

harvesting a *tukang metik*, one who is qualified to divine an auspicious day on which to begin the harvest, is called in. If he decided, for example, that Sunday-*Kliwon* it is to be, then four consecutive Sunday-*Kliwon* later the harvest ceremony takes place and the harvest begins the following day.[18] The ritual from this point on is essentially the same as that described by Kruyt.

In Bali there appear to be only very slight variations in the harvest ceremonies as compared with those held in Java. Liefrinck, writing of rice cultivation in North Bali, remarks that three to five days before harvesting begins a few of the best ears of rice are cut, leaving some stalk and one leaf on each. These are bound together to form the *nini*, the Rice Mother, who is thereupon entered by Śri. When the rice has been gathered in, it is handed over to the women, who attend to all further arrangements. The men are no longer concerned, Liefrinck says, and in general do not even know how much rice is stored, or for what price some may later be sold in the village. When the rice is stored in the barn the *nini* is placed on top of the sheaves, in order that Śri will diffuse her blessing over them.[19]

Grader, writing of rice cultivation in South Bali, notes that in Jembrana, in particular, the period of the New Moon is considered a favourable time to commence the rice harvest. A suitable day on which to make the *nini* is Monday. A handful of unthreshed rice of a certain kind becomes the *nini*, Śri's temporary resting place, and another handful serves as the *nini*'s seat, when she is placed on an offering

---

[18] Geertz, 81.

[19] F.A. Liefrinck, 'Rice Cultivation in Northern Bali', *Bali: Further Studies in Life, Thought, and Ritual*, 1969, 32.

platform of bamboo in the centre of the rice field and presented with fragrant offerings. Harvesting may not begin until two days later, when offerings are again made to Śri within the *nini*, and when she is informed of the farmer's intention to cut the rice.[20] It has already been pointed out elsewhere that to the Javanese farmer, and to the Balinese farmer also, Śri represents the entire rice crop, which is about to suffer the pain of severance by the *ani-ani*, the rice knife. The *nini*, as in Java and other rice-growing areas, is placed with the rice sheaves in the barn after the harvest. A *mantenin* ceremony, a 'rice marriage', is then held for the 'bridal pair', corresponding to the *temanten pari slametan* in Java.[21] The rice barn is decorated with young leaves of the coconut palm, plaited and clipped into elaborate decorations formed with typical Balinese artistry, together with festive poles and coloured cloth. Under no circumstances must the rice be used or sold before the *mantenin*.[22]

It appears from the foregoing that present-day rice ceremonies vary little from the ritual and ceremony observed by Kruyt some fifty years ago, or by van Eerde and others a century or more ago. It is probably safe to say that this ritual, which may be only the surviving remnants of former rituals, is very ancient indeed, probably handed down through countless generations of rice farmers in Java, Bali and other areas of *sawah* cultivation. The fact that Old Javanese was used in *mantras* uttered at some of these ceremonies, as

---

[20] C.J. Grader, 'The Irrigation System of Jĕmbrana', *Bali: Studies in Life, Thought, and Ritual*, 277.

[21] Geertz, 81.

[22] Grader.

well as in the ancient regulations of the ritual cock-fight in Bali, may suggest some original influence stemming from Java, and passing to Bali, Lombok and other places.

RELIGIOUS FESTIVALS OF THE AGRICULTURAL YEAR

In ancient Java there were two major agrarian festivals, the Śrāwana-Bhādra festival in the month of August-September and the Phalguna-Caitra festival held six months later in the month of March-April. Both festivals are mentioned in the *Nāgarakĕrtāgama*[23] but there are much earlier references to be found in Old Javanese inscriptions.[24] These ancient religious festivals were probably originally connected with chthonic community feasts. The name of the goddess worshipped during the Śrāwana-Bhādra festival in Majapahit times is unknown but Pigeaud identifies her with the Southern Ocean goddess, Ratu Lara Kidul, who is also the Goddess of Death. Her prototype in primeval times may have been the Earth Mother, who ruled over the Land of the Dead.[25] In Tantrism, which was also practised in the Majapahit kingdom, Kali, the wife of Śiwa, was worshipped as the Mother.[26] Kali is another name for Durgā, the Goddess of Death.

Unlike the Śrāwana-Bhādra festival, which marked the death or end of the agricultural cycle, before new life is born, the Phālguna-

---

[23] Th. Pigeaud, *Java in the 14th Century*, III, 1960, 9, 10, and IV, 1962, 14.

[24] For example, the copper-plates of Taji, 901 A.D. (H.B. Sarkar, *Corpus of the Inscriptions of Java*, II, 1972, 12.)

[25] Pigeaud IV, 211. In Hayam Wuruk's reign the Śrāwana-Bhādra festival was connected with the cult of deifying the Rajapatni, the Great Royal Lady, the King's grandmother.

[26] See Sister Nivideta, *Kali the Mother*, 1953.

Caitra festival celebrated the harvest, and was a time for venerating the rice goddess Śri, whose bounty had just been gathered in. Caitra was also a time for the farmers to pay their taxes to the ruler; it is mentioned in inscriptions as a time for collecting the 'Lord's due'. In Bali also it was a time for both tax payments and for major festivities from early times.[27] Apart from Śri, the sun god Sūrya still plays a prominent role in the Caitra festival in Bali today, and probably did in ancient Java also; Sūrya was worshipped in Majapahit times and therefore presumably earlier. In former times in Java, and in Bali, the ruler took an active part in the harvest festival celebrations. Court officials and commoners alike played their parts and attendance was compulsory. In more remote rural areas each village celebrated its own festivals, including the harvest celebration, and they continue to do so to the present day.

Apart from the two major festival months of the year, other months also seem to have been occasions for special ceremonial offerings to be presented by the agricultural communities to the ruler, or to some deity of the sanctuaries. The Taji inscription states that in the month of Asuji, at the time of the festival, gold must be offered to the king; the month of Asuji was a month for payment of royal taxes.[28] Kartika was the month in which the image of Buddha in the freehold of Kañcana[29] was to be worshipped

---

[27] Both annual festivals were held in Bali. Liefrinck notes that Cornelis de Houtman referred to them in his account of Bali in 1598. (F.A. Liefrinck, 31.)

[28] Taji copper-plates issued by Balitung in 903 A.D., plate 7 (Sarkar II, 12) and the Kĕlagyan inscription, OJO LXI, 4 and 17.

[29] Kañcana inscription of 860 A.D., plate V, A: line 4, (Sarkar I, 137).

by the people, and at each full moon in the month of Asadha silver and other offerings were to be delivered to the place of purificatory rites.[30] A triennial festival was held in the month of Margasira, at which time one *tahil* of unpolished rice as well as various kinds of fruits were offered to the god Haricandana, and a rice cone, *anna lingga*, to the god Brahma.[31] In the month of Magha festivals were held at which tributes of silver and sacrificial goats were offered to Bhaṭara.[32] There was also a festival in the month of Julung, when flowers were presented to the *patihs* and *carū* offerings were made.[33] The annual festival of *pūja* was also closely connected with the agricultural communities. It appears to have been an occasion on which *pamūja*, 'worship contributions', were collected from the religious residents of a domain by the secular members, as contributions towards the cost of celebrating the festival of *pūja*. References to *pamūja* are found in inscriptions, for example in the Sarwadharma charter issued by the Singasari ruler, Kĕrtanagara.[34]

The *carū* offering mentioned above was apparently the offering of rice strewn on the ground 'to satisfy the lower classes of demons lest they should interfere with the ceremonies'.[35] The earliest

---

[30] Kañcana, plate V, A: line 5.

[31] Bintang Mas inscription of 878 A.D., lines 5-6; Bintang Mas B of 919 A.D., line 4 (Sarkar I, 202, 204, and II, 194).

[32] Palĕpangan (Borobudur) copper-plate of 906 A.D., line 11 (Sarkar II, 58).

[33] Inscription on a Ganeśa image from Singaśari dated 891 A.D., line 13 and the Rubukubu Bhadri copper-plate of 905 A.D., line 3 (Sarkar I, 306 and II, 54).

[34] Sarwadharma charter of 1269 A.D. (Pigeaud, IV, 381-3).

[35] See J.G. de Casparis, *Selected Inscriptions from the 7th to the 9th Century A.D.*, 1956, 242, note 189. Also Sarkar, I, 124, note 131.

reference to *carū* is found in the Dinaya inscription of 760 A.D. wherein we find that *carū* offerings were made during the worship of Agastya, the sage for whose worship the king had an image made 'beautifully prepared ... in black marble'.[36] In the Lintakan copper-plates it is written that King Tuloḍang purchased *sawah* fields and made them freehold in order to furnish the rice for the *carū* offerings to his father's funerary sanctuary.[37] On the occasion of the foundation ceremony connected with land grants, another specific type of offering, the *saji* offering, was made to the deities. This fact is not mentioned in all inscriptions but occurs in many where details are given of the amount offered. For example, in the Taji inscription[38] a list is given of *saji* offerings to the sacred foundation stone, *sang hyang kulumpang*, and to the Fire God Brahma, which include ceremonial cloth and gold. *Saji* offerings appear to have consisted of various foodstuffs as well as gold and silver. Portion of the Kuṭi inscription reads 'There is also the *deśa* named Hnī which will present for *saji* offerings seven bundles (?) of salt, silver 2 *māṣa*, 2 *kupang* with the appearance of Full Moon in in each fourth month'.[39] The Sangguran stone records the presentation of *saji* offerings to *sang makudur*, the officiating priest at the ceremonies.[40]

---

[36] Dinaya stone, OJO I, line 7 (Sarkar, I, 27-8).

[37] Lintakan copper-plates of 919 A.D., I, 1, line 4. (A.B. Cohen Stuart, *Kawi Oorkonden in Facsimile, met Inleiding en Transcriptie*, 1875.

[38] Taji inscription of 903 A.D., plate 3 (Sarkar, II, 9).

[39] Kuṭi inscription, 7B, 3-4 (Sarkar, I, 88).

[40] Sangguran (Minto) stone of 928 A.D., verso, 19-20 (Sarkar, II, 240).

Details are lacking of the sacrificial offerings made at the time of laying the foundation of irrigation works. In Bali, a chicken is buried in the foundation of a new dam, as a sacrifice to the river god, and it can be presumed that a similar sacrifice was made on these occasions in Java; there are no references, in the few inscriptions concerning irrigation works, to any ceremony attached to the laying of the dam foundation. Even in records of the ceremony marking the foundation or confirmation of the establishment of irrigation works, such as the three dams built by the Rakryān Mangibil or Airlangga's Kĕlagyan dam, the inscriptions lack details of offerings made on those occasions. However, there is in the Hariñjing B inscription a reference to 'canal ceremonies' to be held regularly every third day of Caitra, the costs of which must be borne by the village of Wulak.[41]

LAND GRANT CEREMONIES

As has already been remarked, the ties binding the ancient Javanese peasant to his own land were strong indeed. Likewise, a bond existed between a group of farmers and the communal land they owned and worked, or the land on which communal buildings were erected.[42] Therefore, any alteration in the status of land, whether by change of ownership or

---

[41] Hariñjing B inscription, lines 17-18 (van Stein Callenfels, 'De Inscriptie van Sukabumi', *MKAW-L*, 1934, 118).

[42] In Duyvandak's account of the Mentawi Islanders he draws attention to the relationship between these primitive people and their land. For them the act of building a new communal house, an *uma*, has a religious significance; it binds with a mystical bond the people, the material and implements used, and the earth upon which the *uma* stands. The act of building the *uma* is seen as the building of a new world. The *uma* standing on hallowed ground represents to them the centre of the cosmos. (P. Th. Duyvandak, *Inleiding tot de Ethnologie van de Indonesische Archipel*, 1955, 116-17).

by gift deed, usually for religious purposes, was regarded by the rural community as highly significant, especially from a religious point of view.

From Old Javanese charters there is evidence of land having been donated to religious bodies and, less frequently, to guilds who were pledged to donate proceeds from this land to temples and funerary sanctuaries. *Tĕgal* land was converted to *sawah* fields; forests were hewn for new *sawah* land; dry plains, *gaga*, marshlands, *rĕnĕk*, and *sirih*, areca plantations, in fact all kinds of agricultural land, changed hands at some period of time during the Indo-Javanese era, in both Central and East Java. The first known gift of land for religious purposes is recorded in the Plumpungan inscription of 752 A.D.[43] In the second oldest known record of land transaction, the Dinaya stone of 760 A.D.,[44] the ruler made not only a gift of land but of 'well-fed cows and herds of buffalos, with male and female servants ...' for the worship of the sage Agastya.

Not only was *tĕgal* land redeveloped for *sawah*,[45] or new *sawah* fields established, but entire districts were changed in status, becoming freehold districts, or *desa perdikan* as they are now designated, for the upkeep of the religious institutions to which they were assigned. There are charters recording the transfer of land belonging to guilds, such as the 'united body of smiths' or the 'united body of *kalangs*' from its original status to that of a freehold estate. In 907 A.D., for example, the ruler Balitung instigated an

---

[43] See J.G. de Casparis, *Inscripties uit de Çailendra-tijd*, 1950, 9-11.

[44] The Dinaya inscription, line 7 (Sarkar, I, 26-7).

[45] See the Ngabean inscription of 879 A.D. and Ngabean V of 881 A.D., for example (Sarkar, I, 217 and 272).

interesting land transaction when he decreed that a freehold should be created from *sawah* lands and forests as an *anugraha* in favour of the guild of *patihs* and their families, to each *patih* and his family for a period of three years, on a 'share-farming' basis it seems. The reason for the bestowal of this freehold property by the king arose from his desire to reward the *patihs* for faithful service they had rendered at the time of the royal wedding, and for their piety.[46]

Stone and copper-plate charters were treated as tangible evidence of the royal spoken word, which was considered to be the very breathe of magical and spiritual power.[47] These inscribed records of land transactions were revered as sacred objects long after their original consecration and even to the present day they are treated with awe and reverence.[48] Goris, writing of the decennial festival in Bali, gives a very good example of the religious significance attached to inscriptions. He writes:

> After the placing of the offerings the ritual of *wangsuh*, the purification of certain objects regarded as gods, was performed. The deified objects were two inscriptions. One, called Batara Ngĕrati Bumi, written on seven copper sheets, is kept in the Pura Sakti. The other, a more recent text called Ida (or Batara) Ratu Putra, or Ratu Piagĕm, ("Lord Charter"), is kept in the Pura Sakti for the ceremony. During the washing of the inscriptions I was permitted to read the older of the two. It was ... an edict issued by the famous King Jayapangus, all of whose recorded

---

[46] The copper-plates of Mantyāsih (Sarkar, II, 65).

[47] See Selosoemardjan's remarks concerning the Sultan of Yogakarta and the mystical significance attached to his spoken word. Each word the Sultan utters is considered by his people not merely 'spoken by a human tongue, but is divinely inspired and therefore law'. (Selosoemardjan, *Social Changes in Jogjakarta*, 1962, 22f).

[48] See Pigeaud, IV, 483.

pronouncements are, with one exception, identically dated the ninth day after the new moon in the month Crawana ... of the Çaka year 1103 (1181 A.D.).[49]

Goris further remarks:

> It is again apparent that the charter accorded by King Jayapangus is regarded not only as a sacred village relic, but also as a royal, and consequently divine validation of the established system of rights and obligations. The inscription is a tangible proof of divine ... authorization for the village community to exercise the entitlements thereby implied ... there is a general belief that the duties and prohibitions operative in the village were long ago imposed by divine sanction.[50]

With a few exceptions, the terms used in inscriptions where the actual ceremony of land investiture and the consecration ceremony attached to the inscribed stone or copper-plates are concerned, are purely Old Javanese. The exceptions apply to court officials, monetary values, and references to Hindu and Buddhist deities. As Sarkar points out:

> The number of Hindu accessories (used during the foundation ceremony) would not be large even if we included the gift of cloths and gold or silver and cooking pots as parts of the Hindu ritual. No Hindu would however present buffalo-heads and fowls in a religious ceremony. These are often presented, along with other native accessories, and described in pure Javanese terms.[51]

---

[49] Roelof Goris, 'The Decennial Festival in the Village of Selat' in *Bali: Further Studies in Life, Thought, and Ritual*, 117.

[50] Goris, 226, note 62.

[51] H.B. Sarkar, 'Survey of Some Aspects of Old-Javanese Inscriptions of Central Java', in *Studies in Asian History and Culture*, 63.

In the Karangtĕngah inscription[52] recording a grant of land on which a Buddhist sanctuary was to be erected, and *sawah* land for its upkeep, the language recording the actual land grant ceremony is Old Javanese. The names of all participants in the ceremony, including court officials as well, are Indonesian in origin. However, where the establishment of the religious sanctuary itself is described the record is written in Sanskrit. Likewise, in the Pereng inscription,[53] which is also a dual language record, the details of the gift of *sawah* land are recorded in Old Javanese whereas the opening section of the inscription, in praise of Śiwa and the closing four stanzas concerning a religious building, are written in Sanskrit.

There can be little doubt that land grant ceremonies held a religious significance for all those who attended - and the rural community appears to have attended in full force. It is recorded in the Sangguran inscription of 928 A.D. that everyone attended the ceremonial proceedings 'according to their rank, all the *patihs*, the *wahutas, rāmas, kabayan* and the *rāma tpi sering*, the representatives from neighbouring villages. The aged and the young, men and women, from all classes without exception, all attended and partook of the ceremonial food'.[54] The Panggumulan inscription records in detail the elaborate procedure of a land grant ceremony held to commemorate the transfer of village land to *sīma* status in the village of Panggumulan.[55]

---

[52] The Karangtĕngah inscription of 824 A.D. (de Casparis, I, 24-50).

[53] The Wukiran (Pereng) inscription of 862 A.D. (Sarkar, I, 171).

[54] The Sangguran inscription, verso, lines 39-40 (Sarkar, II, 234).

[55] The Panggumulan (Kĕmbang Arum) copper-plates, (Sarkar, II, 24-30).

The order of the foundation ceremony consisted of solemn consecration formulae and the uttering of lurid curses against would-be transgressors of the freehold property then being invested. This was preceded by gift-giving to those taking an official part in the ceremony, and the feasting and entertainment. The ceremonial feasting which followed, and the entertainment, is often described in detail. The Taji copper-plates of 901 A.D., for example, enumerate the various dishes offered for the ceremonial meal and the number of *lontar* leaves distributed to each group of people to place their food upon.[56] An astonishing variety of dishes are mentioned in many inscriptions[57] but, unfortunately, many of the dishes and ingredients listed are unknown to scholars at the present time. However, we can certainly assume that, as sacramental offerings, the dishes would have been prepared with care and elaborately presented and arranged around the sacred stones. Fragrant woods and incense would be burned to waft the 'essence' of the food upwards to the divine spirit of the sacred foundation stone and to the Fire God. The material part of the offering, the actual food, was afterwards eaten by all participants in the ceremony.[58]

After the ceremonial feast everyone joined in the entertainment, which might include dancing for the women, gambling for the men, wild boar and cock-fights, performances by masked players, music and singing, *wayang* performances and recitals of the *Rāmāyaṇa*.[59] This should not

---

[56] Sarkar, II, 4-8.

[57] See the Kĕmbang Arum charter, IIIA, 18-19 (Sarkar, II, 37).

[58] The Ngabean copper-plate of 879 A.D. (Sarkar, I, 223).

[59] See F.H. van Naerssen, 'Twee Koperen Oorkonden van Balitung in het Koloniaal Instituut te Amsterdam Holland', *BKI*, XCV, 1937, 445.

be thought of merely as entertainment in the modern sense of the word, but as possessed of religious significance as well, in the same way as the ceremonial feasting. Just as the food would have been beautifully arranged as an offering to the sacred stone and to Brahma, so may the dance have been for the pleasure of the deities. The blood spilt at the cock-fight was a symbolic sacrifice, perhaps to guard against evil spirits attempting to interfere with the solemnity of the consecration ritual which followed the entertainment.[60] Mask dances not only portray acts of magic and comedy but divine intervention as well. The religious significance of the *wayang* and the role of the *Rāmāyaṇa* in the instruction of moral codes and behaviour is well known.

Following the entertainment, the participants in the ceremony of land investiture turned their attention to the solemn ritual of the consecration of the foundation or inscription stone. According to some inscriptions both men and women first prepared themselves with ceremonial dress, flowers, and paint, before taking up their appointed positions, then they 'sat on the ground in a circle, with the face turning to *hyang kudur* [the officiating priest] and the sacred *sīma watu kulumpang* [the foundation stone], which was placed under the canopy in the middle of the ... ground'.[61] When all were seated '*sang makudur* uttered the oath formula, cut off (the neck) of the hen which was crushed on the sacred *kulumpang*, threw off the egg on the *watu sīma*, and uttered oaths ....'[62] He called upon the gods and the various spirits, both indigenous and Indian, to witness the foundation of the

---

[60] See below concerning cock-fighting.

[61] Sarkar II, 28, line 12.

[62] The Sangsang copper-plates of 907 A.D., verso, lines 1-2 (Sarkar, II, 95). The formula of an Old Javanese oath of 931 A.D. was still used in Bali in 1859. Hendrik Kern, *Verspreide Geschriften*, VI, 1917, 308.

sīma, the freehold land, and to protect it for time everlasting, *tka dlaha ning dlaha*. The spirits invoked at this time included ancestors. In the Mantyāsih copper-plate of 907 A.D., for example, the *makudur* called upon 'those dead and deified beings of earlier times', the former rulers of Mataram, commencing with the founder Sañjaya.[63]

The god Brahma was also invoked and, before the *makudur* uttered the curses against those who might trespass or interfere with the *sīma* in any way, Brahma was placed on the sacred stone. The foundation stone was revered and valued far above Brahma; the Taji inscription records that the stone was presented with offerings of four sets of ceremonial cloth and four gold *māsa*, whereas the god Brahma only received one set of cloth (a *kain* and a headcloth) and one *māsa*.

The curse formula was a significant part of the ceremony attached to land investiture, dating from early times; the earliest occurrence of the oaths and curses which featured in most charters thereafter is found in Śri Kahulunan's inscription of 842 A.D.[64] Sarkar draws attention to the fact that in the Kalasan charter of 778 A.D. and the Kĕlurak charter of 782 A.D., all future kings were requested, by way of the words inscribed on the stone which was to last forever, to protect the domains and institutions for posterity. These inscriptions seem to be the last ones to place reliance on the protection of future rulers alone. For the protection of freeholds against trespassers and unauthorized tax collectors additional measures were apparently

---

63 The Mantyāsih copper-plates I, lines 7-9, (Sarkar, II, 68).

64 The inscription of Śri Kahulunan (de Casparis, I, 79-95). The Kuṭi copper-plates of 840 A.D. (Sarkar, I, 81-3), two years earlier than Śri Kahulunan's inscription, contains lengthy curse formulae; however, this inscription is considered to properly belong to the Majapahit period, since Majapahit is mentioned. The inclusion of no less than twenty-eight lines of curses may suggest troubled times.

considered necessary.[65] Thus, a curse formula was inserted into subsequent charters, calculated to strike terror into the hearts of those who would defy the prohibitions set down therein.

Curses uttered by the officiating priest, who was neither Hindu nor Buddhist, were designed to deter the most intrepid wrongdoer, and were apparently considered so efficacious that they were carried on down through the centuries. Some must have indeed been terrifying for the listener as, for example, the curse hurled by the *makudur* at the Sangguran ceremony:

> ... whoever disturbs the village at Sangguran ... he may be brought to destruction .... He may be killed by all the gods in such a way that he may not (find time to) turn behind, he may not (find time to) look behind: he may be pushed in the front-side; struck on the left side, his mouth may be struck, his forehead may be battered, his belly may be ripped open, his intestines may be rooted out, his entrails may be drawn out, his heart may be plucked out, his flesh may be eaten, his blood may be drunk up, then he may be trampled upon, lastly he may be killed! [66]

Some of the curses uttered included threats aptly applicable to an irrigation society as, for example, a curse that the wrongdoer may be overtaken by the fate of being 'dipped in the waters of the dam'[67] - surely an understatement - or the horrifying end to be brought about by being 'crushed between the stones of the dike'.[68] It may be assumed that the culprit was to replace the sacrificial chicken at the base of a new dam. Although expressed with typical Old Javanese economy of words, these threats may possibly have caused a would-be

---

[65] See Sarkar, I, 111, note 96.

[66] The Sangguran inscription, lines 29-33 (Sarkar's translation, II, 241).

[67] The Sugih Manik charter (Sarkar, II, 156).

[68] The Wuatan Tija inscription, (Sarkar, I, 258).

transgressor to have second thoughts. However, apparently in later times even curses were found insufficient as a deterrent, and fines too were laid down.

Sarkar remarks that:

> It is not easy to explain why the foundation ceremonies present a mixed pattern of Hindu and Indonesian rituals .... If a guess can be hazarded, the mixture of rituals in the foundation-ceremonies is due to the *susu-kulumpang*, which outwardly looked like a linga, but was in reality a descendant and representative of the prehistoric menhir. Obviously, it has to be pacified and worshipped with Indonesian accessories, to which Indian elements were added as Indian gods were also invoked. The spirits of ancestors, who used to descend on the pre-Hindu menhirs, descended on the *susu-kulumpang*, and their traces have been left over in the curse-formulae for the protection of the freehold and, in some cases, of the kingdom.[69]

The prevalence of menhirs and similar stone shafts which were widely revered as the seats of ancestral spirits when they were invoked[70] facilitated the adoption of Śiwa *linggas*. Wheatley, writing of similar stone shafts in Vietnam, says that:

> There can be little doubt that the menhir was originally a spirit-stone, a material manifestation of a chthonic god who was himself a divinisation of the energy of the earth ... and in some areas was eventually transformed, under Sivaite influence, into the *liṅga* that symbolised the permanent and imperishable principal of the Hinduised state.[71]

---

[69] Sarkar, 'Survey of Some Aspects of Old-Javanese Inscriptions of Central Java', in *Studies in Asian History and Culture*, 1970, 63. The stone *lingga* in conjunction with the *yoni*, the symbolic female element, served in other forms of agricultural ritual. Water poured over the *lingga-yoni* symbol flowed down into the earth, thereby fertilizing it.

[70] See J.L. Swellengrebel, 'Introduction' to *Bali: Studies in Life, Thought, and Ritual*, 28, concerning this aspect of ancestor worship in Indonesia.

[71] Paul Wheatley, *Agricultural Terracing*, 1965, 136.

The *watu sīma*, the stone mentioned with the *kulumpang*,[72] was apparently in the form of a *lingga*. Buchari, writing of the inscribed *lingga* of Rambianak, remarks that these small columns or *linggas* were used as 'boundary posts', to mark the borders of freehold *sawah* fields. The Rambianak inscription contains the phrase *sinusuknya ya watu sīma sradi*, 'It [the *sawah*] was afterwards marked with *sīma* stones at all corners'.[73] An inscribed *lingga* recently found in Central Java, which records a *sīma sawah* of four *tampahs*,[74] is probably one of the four originally serving the same purpose. Besides the stone *linggas* used to denote border limits Ganeśa images were placed at certain points, apparently as 'guardians', to protect places considered to be dangerous, such as the confluence of two large rivers or open *tĕgal* fields subject to trespassers. An example in the latter case is found in the inscribed Ganeśa from Singasari.[75]

THE RELIGIOUS SIGNIFICANCE OF COCK-FIGHTING

Cock-fighting is mentioned in Old Javanese inscriptions among the various forms of entertainment held before the consecration of the sacred foundation stone at landgrant ceremonies. In one inscription, recording the invocation to ancestral spirits, the priest calls upon

---

[72] The exact difference between the foundation stones *watu sīma*, *sīma watu kulumpang* and *susu kulumpang* is not clear. In the case of *susu kulumpang* the *k* is dropped from *susuk* (see Sarkar, II, 41, note 83).

[73] M. Boechari, 'An Inscribed Liṅga from Rambianak', *BEFEO*, XLIX, 1959, 408.

[74] M. Soekarto Kartoatmodjo, 'The Discovery of Three New Inscriptions in the District of Klaten (South Central Java)' in *Bulletin of the Archaeological Institute of the Republic of Indonesia, No.8*, Djakarta, 1969, 18-22.

[75] Inscription of Balingwan of 891 A.D. (Sarkar, I, 305).

'... deified beings of earlier times who ... arranged the fight (of cocks and boars) in the foundation region ....'[76] Apparently cock-fighting was also a source of royal revenue. It is stated in the Kĕlagyan inscription that 'from the proceeds of the cock-fight, amounting to one *māsa* and two *kupang*, one *māsa* shall be deducted for the king's revenue'.[77] In Majapahit times, when during the dry season the King and his Court went on pilgrimages to sacred places an important item on the itinerary were the cock-fights. In the *Nāgarakĕrtāgama* it reads:

2. There is a cultivated area called Sīma, south of Jalagiri, going eastward from the Royal compound.

3. pleasantly lively, for it is a place for vows of the public, at the time of the cock-fights; therefore it is (visited) uninterruptedly.[78]

In Bali, cock-fighting is still included in ceremonial affairs, for whereas the colonial period saw the end of cock-fighting in Java, the government did not succeed in suppressing it there. Although cock-fighting appears to have been a popular pastime from ancient times, a pastime in which the Court and the rural communities both took part, it had on the other hand a religious significance. Originally cock-fighting served as a preliminary to temple feasts. Liefrinck, discussing the *subak* harvest festival in Bali, refers to the cock-fight held in the courtyard of the temple. It was compulsory for each rice farmer to attend with a certain number of

---

[76] The Mantyāsih I copper-plate of 907 A.D., B7 (Sarkar, II, 75).

[77] OJO. LXI, line 6.

[78] The *Nāgarakĕrtāgama*, canto 17, stanza 4, lines 2-3 (Pigeaud, III, 21).

birds, proportionate to the number of his *sawah* fields. Those farmers who failed to attend the contests, and the unfortunate ones whose cocks refused to fight, were fined. The fines and the percentage levy on stake money helped to defray the costs of the *subak* festival.[79]

Van Eck has translated and published an old *sima tetajen*, a document of rules and regulations relating to the cock-fight.[80] The document, although found in Bali, was written in Old Javanese with a sprinkling of Balinese words, and includes the words 'this *sima* is a gift from the King of Wilatikta (Majapahit)' which van Eck considers proof of the Old Javanese origin of this *sima tetajen*. The regulations contained in the *sima tetajen* are not arranged in any order or sequence which, van Eck remarks, is usually the case with genuine *adat* documents. The contents are expressed in a style of typical Old Javanese understatement, and points which were probably considered obvious are omitted altogether. Van Eck has filled in the details of the contest from actual eyewitness accounts and a brief summary of his account follows.

To outsiders the religious significance of cock-fighting seems to have been little known or understood. The participants in a contest feel that the gods will descend and be present if the contest is held in the immediate vicinity of a temple. The participants never neglect to present their offerings to the various gods in the cock-fight arena. Offerings are in the form of an *ampilan*, a box bound around with unspun cotton, and filled with rice, *sirih*, coins and so on, as a humble gift to the gods in order to gain their blessing on

---

[79] Liefrinck, 'Rice Cultivation in Northern Bali' in *Bali: Further Studies in Life, Thought, and Ritual*, 37.

[80] R. van Eck, 'Schetsen uit het volksleven in Nederlandsch Oost-Indië, *De Indische Gids*, I, i, 1879, 102-18.

the contest. The cocks, fighting to the death, are seen as atonement offerings to the gods as their blood is shed upon the soil.

Cock-fighting was organized not only at the local level, but at the state level by the ruler.[81] *Tetajen lewih* were held in the *kraton* and participation in these contests was seen as *buat haji*, a duty to the ruler. Besides providing fighting cocks each participant was required to have a certain sum of money to enable him to place bets. The only persons not permitted to take part in these bouts were the priests. Attendance for others was compulsory but seldom did the ruler compel his subjects to attend. Enrolment to attend the *tetajen lewih* was usually made with the district head and the contest continued for at least two months, beginning each day at midday and finishing at nightfall.

Contests at district level took place at the district centre, under local government control. Instead of permission to hold the fight issuing from the ruler it came from the *punggawa*, the district head. The same rules and regulations applied but fines were less severe and the contests continued only for one month. Cock-fighting at the village level, *tetajen desa*, was held annually, the major rule being that it must be held in the immediate vicinity of the village temple. Temple servants shared the taxes and proceeds of the fines with the village head. Every villager was required to attend with two fighting cocks and was fined if he failed to do so. The *tetajen subak* took place after the rice harvest and only members of *subak* associations were permitted to take part. The contest was held next to the *subak* temple. Van Eck was told by *subak* members that they participated in the contest not so much for pleasure as for the purpose of offering a small measure of thanks

---

[81] Van Eck was writing in 1879.

and gratitude to the deities who had filled their rice barns with valuable grain.

The *juru kemong*, the 'head of the arena', who was in charge of the contest, uses a *kemong*, a metal drum, to control the fight. Every stroke of the *kemong* represents one or other of the *sima tetajen* rules or regulations, whichever might apply to the fight at that moment. Van Eck gives a translation of the forty-five articles of rules contained in the *sima tetajen*. They not only give some indication of the importance of the pastime for the Balinese, but also some indication of the religious significance cock-fighting must have held for the ancient Javanese rural community as well. The *sima* closes with the utterance of a curse, 'all those who violate this *sima tetajen* shall bring down upon their heads the wrath of the gods, and they shall be visited by all manner of grievous ills and misfortune'.

TEMPLES AND BATHING SANCTUARIES

On the summits and slopes of extinct volcanic mountains in Central and East Java ruins of ancient terrace sanctuaries have been found. There are traces of terrace buildings in the Kali Pikatan area on the slopes of the Welirang mountain and the Anjasmoro Ranges, which appear to belong to a pre-Indian period,[82] and which can probably be compared with the ancient terrace complex in the Gio-Linh province of Vietnam, discussed by Wheatley.

Wheatley considers it possible that the upper terraces of the Gio-Linh complex may have been connected with the cult of the mountain god. He also remarks that 'The water seeping from the sacred hill and carrying the subtle energies of the divinity to the villages and fields

---

[82] See N.J. Krom, *Inleiding tot de Hindoe-Javaansche Kunst*, II, 1923, 350-53.

below also finds analogues in other parts of Southeast Asia ... and there are numerous Javanese examples ...'[83] Stutterheim similarly describes the Jalaṭunda bathing place noting that the water appears to have flowed from the top of the sacred mountain Penanggungan, through a system of channels and basins, to finally flow out over the land. Stutterheim sees Jalaṭunda as a terrace sanctuary for the worship of ancestors as well as of the mountain god. It is possible, however, that it was closely connected with irrigation.[84]

Rivers are considered sacred and in ancient Java were referred to as *sang hyang*, holy or sacred; in Balitung's Wanagiri charter the Kali Solo is called *sang hyang* Mahawan and Siṇḍok's inscription of 943 A.D. refers to the river as *luah prasiddha*, the sacred river. De Casparis points out that in both cases the inscriptions are referring to the river in connection with a religious sanctuary or temple, a *dhārma kamulān*.[85] There are actual records of rivers having been diverted to flow past, or through, the temple. Raka Pikatan of Central Java directed that the course of the Kali Opak be diverted so that its waters should flow past the *tirtha*, the sacred bathing place; it is recorded that 'After the Çiva sanctuary had been completed in its divine splendour, the (course of the) river was changed so that it rippled along the grounds ... [of the sanctuary]'.[86]

---

[83] Wheatley, 137.

[84] According to Palerm there are still great irrigation works in Mexico which are thought to have been the ruler's resort. (Angel Palerm, 'The agricultural basis of urban civilization in Mesoamerica' in Julian Steward and others, *Irrigation Civilizations*, 1955, 36.). This may apply to Jalaṭunda, and Candi Rejo in the Kali Pikatan area.

[85] See de Casparis, I, 149, note 1.

[86] De Casparis, II, 328.

A fragment of bas-relief from ancient Majapahit depicts a river flowing through what appears to be a temple and thence to the nearby *sawah* fields.[87] There can be no doubt that the intention here was to divert water intended for irrigation of the *sawah* fields to flow through a consecrated place, in order that the water should be endowed with life-giving qualities. It seems that a religious structure, a temple or a sanctuary of some kind, was always erected and a supporting freehold established, to commemorate the founding of an irrigation project, or the extension of an existing *sawah* complex. On the slopes of the Kelud, for example, there are remains of a sanctuary possibly built to commemorate the Hariñjing dam. An investigation may bring to light other examples, but for the present the relationship between archaeological remains of sanctuaries and centres of *sawah* culture belonging to kingdoms long dead must remain supposition.

---

[87] See A.J. Bernet Kempers, *Ancient Indonesian Art*, plate 288.

CONCLUSIONS

The pattern of development of *sawah* cultivation during the Indo-Javanese period appears consistent with Adam's and Collier's theories of hydraulic development referred to in Chapters Two and Three. *Sawah* cultivation, directed by the ruler or by religious bodies, was based on a foundation of purely indigenous irrigation organization already established before the arrival of Indian influence. This conclusion is supported by the fact that all agricultural terms, as well as the titles of various rural officials are Javanese and occur in inscriptions dating from the earliest period of Indianization. The communal nature of the Javanese village, with its stress on mutual assistance, lent itself to the development of farming co-operation and village federation for the purpose of efficient irrigation management.

The development of *sawah* cultivation in Central Java during the earlier part of the Indo-Javanese period and in East Java during the entire Indo-Javanese period to the fifteenth century, can be traced through Old Javanese inscriptions. It is possible to trace the development and extension of major rice-growing areas in ancient Java by i) the number and distribution of inscriptions concerning land grants, ii) the presence of temples and other sanctuaries in association with inscriptions, and iii) the duplication of place-names, a phenomenon which occurs not only within both Central and East Java but between the two regions, thus indicating the expansion by the court and by religious bodies into outlying undeveloped regions. It can also be concluded that earlier migrations from established villages to nearby uncultivated areas took place, due to population expansion beyond the village capacity. Names of the mother villages were perpetuated in the new areas.

It is evident that East Java played a prominent part in the development of wet-rice cultivation in ancient Java. The establishment and continuity of the major rice-growing regions of East Java is revealed in the inscriptions of the period. For example, the irrigation installation mentioned in the Hariñjing charter at the beginning of the ninth century comes to our attention again in the Kandangan edict of the mid-fourteenth century, where it is recorded that the original dam had been repaired. The Bakalan inscription reveals a link between the tenth century *sawah*-based region of Mangibil and the fourteenth century kingdom of Majapahit, through the extension of the water supply flowing from the Pikatan River into the Brangkal. Evidence of the extent to which Mpu Sindok's original centre of irrigation spread can be found five and a half centuries later; in the Sarangan inscription of 929 A.D. are place-names found also in the Trailokyapuri stone of 1486 A.D. Likewise, Airlangga's inscription of 1037 A.D. lists important *sawah* areas which appear again in the Suradakan copper-plates of 1447 A.D.

No specific term has been found in the inscriptions to prove the existence of irrigation associations independent of village administration, such as the Balinese *sekaha subaks*. However, there is some tentative indication of similar organization; for example, in Bali the *sekaha subaks* are given names, usually signifying a connection with water, which are similar to Old Javanese names (such as Talang Air) found in land grant charters. These denote the proximity of water and possibly the existence of irrigation works of importance. In nineteenth century Java it was usual that, where fields owned by *sawah* farmers were situated in a certain area even though the owners belonged to different villages, this area was given a name. In the light of this perhaps a closer study may reveal that place-names occurring in inscriptions refer to areas belonging to irrigation guilds and not to villages as assumed. Finally, the term *hulair karamān* which occurs in some charters may apply to a council of irrigation heads, or to an association of heads.

The Bakalan inscription is pertinent to the question of *sawah* co-operation in ancient Java since it may represent a type of early *kerta sima subak*; there are parallels between the *rakryān's* decree and *subak* regulations concerning water distribution, guarding the dam against vandals, and the punishment of those who defy prohibitions or commit other breaches of the regulations laid down. In both cases mention is made of fines to be levied and the fixed time for payment. It is also possible that the officials mentioned in the inscriptions were the *'sedahan agung'* the *sedahan tembaku'* and the *'klian subak'* respectively. However, whichever type of irrigation administration applied, the fact remains that in ancient Java there existed a well-managed system of hydraulic organization, enabling the development of extensive *sawah*-based kingdoms during the Indo-Javanese period, reaching the peak of florescence in the Majapahit era.

The irrigation works built by the Bhagawanta Bāri, by Rakryān Mangibil and by the rulers Siṇḍok and Airlangga lie in ruins, but a millennium after, in the present time new hydraulic projects are being established in the same places, at Briti and at Slawe as well as on the ancient Hariñjing site, and at Karangkates. Meanwhile, the Hariñjing, Bakalan and Kĕlagyan sacred inscription stones still exist to proclaim the original irrigation installations, which played their role in the long history of Javanese *sawah* cultivation.

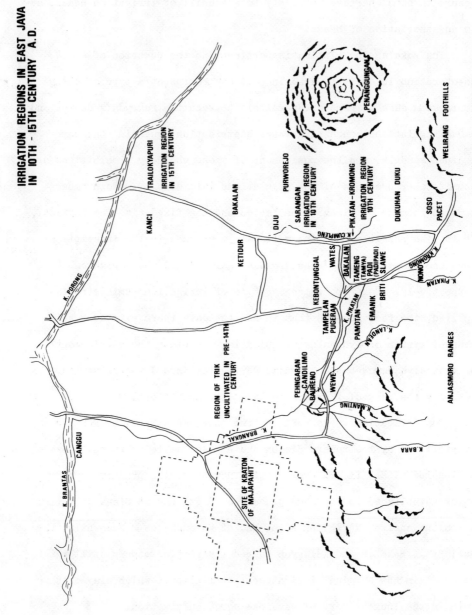

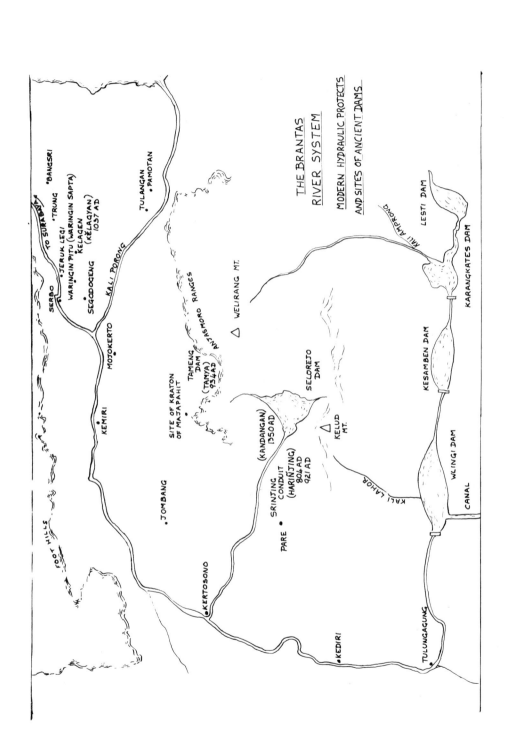

LIST OF ABBREVIATIONS

BKI	*Bijdragen tot de Taal-, Land- en Volkenkunde van Nederlandsch-Indië uitgegeven door het Koniklijk Instituut voor Taal-, Land- en Volkenkunde*
BEFEO	*Bulletin de l'École française d'Extrême-Orient*
De Casparis I	Casparis, J.G. de, *Inscripties uit de Çailendra-tijd, Prasasti² dari zaman Çailendra*, Bandung, 1950.
De Casparis II	Casparis, J.G. de, *Selected Inscriptions from the 7th to the 9th Century A.D.*, Bandung, 1956.
Feestbundel	*Feestbundel uitgegeven door Koninklijk Bataviaasch Genootschap van Kunsten en Wetenschappen bij gelegenheid van zijn 150-jarig bestaan*
MKAW-L	*Mededeelingen van het Koninklik Nederlandsch Akademie van Wetenschappen, afdeeling Letterkunde*
MNZG	*Mededeelingen vanwege het Nederlandsch Zendinggenootschap*
OJO	Krom, N.J. (ed.), *Oud-Javaansche oorkonden: Nagelaten transcripties van wijlen Dr J.L.A. Brandes, VBG*, LX, 1913
OV	*Oudheidkundig verslag, Oudheidkundige Dienst in Nederlandsch-Indië*
POD	*Oudheidkundige Dienst in Nederlandsch-Indië, Publicaties*
TAG	*Tijdschrift van het Nederlandsch Aardrijkskundig Genootschap*
TBG	*Tijdschrift voor Indische Taal-, Land- en Volkenkunde uitgegeven door het Bataviaasch Genootschap van Kunsten en Wetenschappen*
VBG	*Verhandelingen van Koninklijk Bataviaasch Genootschap van Kunsten en Wetenschappen*

BIBLIOGRAPHY

Adams, Robert M., 'Developmental stages in Ancient Mesopotamia', in Julian H. Steward and others, *Irrigation Civilizations: a comparative study*. Social Science Monographs I, Washington, 1955

Adatrechtbundels, XV, 1918 and XXXIII, 1930, The Hague

Akkeren, Philip van, *Sri and Christ. A study of the Indigenous Church in East Java*, London, 1970

Alisjahbana, S. Takdir, *Indonesia: Social and Cultural Revolution*, Kuala Lumpar, 1951

Atmodjo, M.M. Sukarto K., 'Preliminary Report on a Copper-plate Inscription of Asuhduren', *BKI*, CXXVI, 1970, 215-27

Barrett, A.M., 'Two old copperplate inscriptions of Balitung', unpublished M.A. thesis, University of Sydney, 1968

Bataviaasche Genootschap van Kunsten en Wetenschappen. Notulen van de algemeene en directie vergaderingen, 1888, xiii and 12

Bernet Kempers, August Johan, *Ancient Indonesian art*, Amsterdam, 1959

Beyer, H. Otley, 'The Origin and History of the Philippine Rice Terraces', *Proceedings of the Eighth Pacific Science Congress*, Quezon City, 1953, I

Birkelbach, Aubrey N., *Jr.*, 'The Subak Association', *Indonesia*, 16 (October) 1973, 153-69.

Bosch, F.D.K., 'Inventaris der Hindoe-oudheden op den grondslag van Dr R.D.M. Verbeek's oudheden van Java' Report No. 1698. *Oudheidkundige Dienst van Nederlansch-Indië, Rapporten*, Pt II, 1915, 207

____, 'De oorkonde van Kembang Aroem', *OV*, 1925, Bijl.B, 41-9

____, 'Uit de grensgebieden tussen Indische Invloedsfeer en Oudinheems volksgeloof op Java', *BKI*, CX, 1954

____, *Selected Studies in Indonesian Archaeology*, The Hague, 1961

Brandes, J.L.A., 'Een Jayapattra, of acte van rechterlijke uitspraak van Çaka 849', *TBG*, XXXII, 1889, 98-149

Brandes, J., 'Een oud-Javaansch Alphabet van Midden-Java', *TBG*, XXXII, 1889, 441-54

Boechari, 'A preliminary note on the study of the Old Javanese civil administration' in *Studies in Asian History, Proceedings of the Asian History Congress*, 1961, London, 1969.

Boechari, M., 'An Inscribed Liṅga from Rambianak', *BEFEO*, XLIX, 1959
    405-08

Buchari, 'Epigraphy and Indonesian Historiography', in Soedjatmoko (ed.),
    An Introduction to Indonesian Historiography, New York, 1965, 48-73.

Casparis, J.G., de, *Inscripties uit de Çailendra-tijd. Prasasti^2
    dari zaman Çailendra*, Bandung, 1950

_____, *Selected Inscriptions from the 7th to the 9th Century A.D.*,
    Bandung, 1956

_____, 'Historical Writings on Indonesian (Early Period), in
    D.G.E. Hall (ed.), *Historians of South East Asia*, London, 1961
    121-63

_____, *Indonesian Palaeography, A History of Writing in Indonesia
    from the Beginnings to c. A.D. 1500*, Handbuch der Orientalistik,
    lll Abt.: Indonesian, Malaysia und die Philippinen, Leiden/Koln,
    1975

Chang, Chih-Kwang, *The Archaeology of Ancient China*, (Revised and
    enlarged edition), New Haven and London, 1968

Clason, E.W.H., *Afschrift nota over het stelsel van waterbeheer en
    gewoon onderhoud in vervand met de instituut der oeloe-oeloe
    pembagian*, Jakarta, 1971

Claesson, H.J.M., 'Despotism and Irrigation', *BKI*, CXXIX, 1973, 70-85

Coedès, George, *The Indianized States of Southeast Asia*, (ed. by
    W.F. Vella, trans. by S.B. Cowing), Canberra, 1968

Cohen, Stuart A.B., *Kawi Oorkonden in Facsimile, met Inleiding en
    Transcriptie*, Leiden, 1875

Collier, Donald, 'Development of civilization on the coast of Peru'
    in Julian H. Steward and others, *Irrigation Civilizations:
    a comparative study*, Social Science Monographs I, Washington, 1955

Coulborn, Rushton, *The Origin of Civilized Societies*, Princeton, N.J.,
    1969

Damais, L.-Ch., 'Epigrafische aantekeningen', *TBG*, LXXXIII, 1949,
    1-26

_____, 'Pre-seventeenth-Century Indonesian History: Sources and
    Directions', in Soedjatmoko (ed.), *An Introduction to Indonesian
    Historiography*, New York, 1965

_____, 'Études d'epigraphie indonésienne: III, Liste des principales
    inscriptions datées de l'Indonésie', *BEFEO*, XLVI, 1952-4, 1-105,
    with appendices

_____, *Répertoire Onomastique de l'Épigraphie Javanaise ... Étude
    d'Epigraphie Indonésienne*, LXVI, Paris, 1970

Daw Thin Kyi, Dr, 'Arakanese Capitals: a Preliminary Survey of Their Geographical Siting', *Journal of the Burma Research Society*, LIII, 2, Dec. 1970

Dobby, E.H.G., *Southeast Asia* (10th edn), London, 1969

Durkeim, Émile, *The Division of Labour in Society* (trans. by G. Simpson), New York, 1965

Duyvendak, J. Ph., *Inleiding tot de Ethnologie van de Indonesische Archipel*, vijfde druk, Djakarta, 1955

Echols, John, *An Indonesian-English Dictionary* (by J.M. Echols and H. Shaddily) (2nd edn), New York, 1963

Eck, R. van, 'Schetsen uit het volksleven van Nederlandsch Oost-Indië. Het hanenvecht'. *De Indische Gids*, I, 1, Jan. 1879, 102-118

Eck, R. van and F.A. Liefrinck, 'Kerta-Sima of Gemeente-en Waterschappen-wetten op Bali. Inleiding', *TBG*, XXIII, 1876, 161-5

_____, 'Vertaling van de Kerta Sima Soebak of waterschappenwetten', *TBG*, XXIII, 1876, 224-57

Eerde, J.C. van, 'Gebruiken bij den Rijstbouw en Rijstoogst op Lombok', *TBG*, XLV, 1902, 563-74

Encyclopaedie van Nederlansch-Indie, met medewerking van verschillende geleerden ambtenaren en officieren samengesteld door J. Paulus, I, 's Gravenhage, 1917

Faille, P. de Roo de la, 'Irrigatie en Agrarische Toestanden in West Lombok', *Adatrechtbundel*, XV, 1918, Serie U, no.19, 178-260

Fisher, Charles A., *South-East Asia: a social, economic and political geography* (2nd edn), London, 1965

_____, 'A View of South-east Asia', in R.L. Singh (*ed.*), *Rural Settlements in Monsoon Asia*, Varanasi-5, 1972, 1-15

Fischer, H. Th., *Inleiding tot de Culturele Anthropologie van Indonesia*, derde druk, Haarlem, 1952

Forbes, R.J., *Studies in Ancient Technology*, II (2nd rev. edn), Leiden, 1965

Fukuo, Euno, 'Rural Settlements and Rice Harvest in Java from the standpoint of socio-economic Rural Geography', in R.L. Singh (*ed*), *Rural Settlements in Monsoon Asia*, Varanasi-5, 1972

Geertz, C., *Agricultural Involution: the Processes of Ecological Change*, Berkeley and Los Angeles, 1963

_____, *The Religion of Java*, London, 1964

Gericke, J.F.C. and T. Roorda, *Javaansch-Nederlansch handwoordenboek*. Verm. en. verb. door A.C. Vreede, met medewerking van J.G.H. Gunning, 2 vols. Amsterdam, 1901

Gonda, J., *Sanskrit in Indonesia* (2nd edn), Sata-Pitaka Series, Indo-Asian Literatures, XCIX, New Delhi, 1973

Gonggrijp, G., *Schets eener economische geschiedenis van Indonesië*, Haarlem, 1928

Goris, Roelof, *Prasasti Bali*, I and II, Bandung, 1954

_____, *Ancient History of Bali* (rev. edn), Den Pasar, 1965

_____, 'The Decennial Festival in the Village of Selat', in *Bali: Further Studies in Life, Thought, and Ritual*, The Hague, 1969

Gorkom, K.W., van, 'Het water op Java, in betrekking tot den landbouw', *De Indische Gids*, I, 1, Jan. 1879, 545-84

Grader, G.J., 'The Irrigation System in the Region of Jĕmbrana', in *Bali: Life, Thought, and Ritual*, The Hague and Bandung, 1960

_____, 'The State Temples of Mengwi', in *Bali: Life, Thought, and Ritual*, The Hague and Bandung, 1960, 155-86

Groeneman, I., *De Garĕbĕgs te Ngajogyakărtă met photogrammen van Cephas*, s'Gravenhage, 1895

Groeneveldt, W.P., *Historical Notes on Indonesia and Malaya. Compiled from Chinese Sources*, Djakarta, 1960

Groothoff, A., 'Studie over het inlandsche waterschapwezen (soebakwezen) op Bali en Lombok', *Adatrechtbundel*, 15, 1918 Bijl, A, Serie U, no. 27, 341-52

Groslier, B. Ph., *Angkor et le Camboge au XVIe siècle d'auprès les sources portugaises et espagnoles*, Paris, 1958

_____, 'Our Knowledge of Khmer Civilization, a reappraisal', *Journal of the Siam Society*, XLVIII, 1, June 1960, 1-28

Gunawardhana, R.A.L., 'Irrigation and Hydraulic Society in Ancient and Early Medieval Ceylon', paper presented at the 28th Congress of Orientalists, Canberra, 1971, Special Congress Seminars: Irrigation Civilizations

Haar, Barend ter, *Adat Law in Indonesia* (trans. and ed. by A.A. Shiller and E.A. Hoebel), Djakarta, 1962

Hagan, R.M. and others (eds), *Irrigation of Agricultural Lands*, Agronomy Series No. 11, American Society of Agronomy, Wisconsin, 1967

Hall, Kenneth R. and John K. Whitmore (ed), *Explorations in early Southeast Asian history: The origins of Southeast Asian statecraft*, Michigan papers on South and Southeast Asia, No.11, 1976

Hanks, Lucien Mason, *Rice and Man: agricultural ecology in Southeast Asia*, Chicago, 1972

Happé, P.L.E., 'Eene beschouwing over het Zuid-Balische soebakwezen en zijn verwording in verband met de voorgenomen vorming van waterschappen in Ned.-Indië'- *De Indische Gids*, XLI, 1, 1919, 183-200

Heekeren, H.R. van, *The Stone Age of Indonesia* (2nd rev. edn with a contribution by R.P. Soejono), The Hague, 1972

Heine-Geldern, Robert, 'Conceptions of State and Kingship in Southeast Asia', Data paper No.18, Southeast Asia Program, Department of Far Eastern Studies, New York, 1956

Hinloopen Labberton, D. van, 'Oud-Javanaase gegevens omtrent de vulkanologie van Java', *Djawa*, 1st Jaargang, no.3, 1921

Ho, Robert, 'Environment, Man and Development', inaugural lecture, University of Malaysia, 1962

Holle, K.F., *Tabel van Oud-en Nieuw-Indische Alphabetten. Bijdragen tot de Palaeographie van Nederlansch-Indië*, s'Hage, 1882

Hooijer, C.R., 'Indonesian Prehistoric Tools. A Catalogue of the Houbolt Collection', in J.E. van Lohuizen-De Leeuw (ed.), *Studies in South Asian Culture*, II, Leiden, 1969

Hughes Buller, E., 'Gabrbands in Baluchistan', in *Archaelogical Survey of India*, Annual Report 1903-04, Calcutta, 1906

Jansz, Pieter, *Practisch Javaansch-Nederlandsch woordenboek: met Latijnsche karakters. Bewerkt en voorgezet door P. Ant. Jansz*, Tweede druk, Semarang, 1913

Jay, Robert R., *Religion and Politics in Rural Central Java*, Cultural Report Series No.12, Southeast Asia Studies, Yale University, New Haven, Conn., 1963

_____, *Javanese Villagers. Social Relations in Rural Modjokuto*, Cambridge, Mass. 1969

Junghuhn, F.W., *Java*, II, Tweede verbeterde uitgave, 1954, Amsterdam, 1850

Juynboll, H.H., *Oudjavaansch-Nederlandsche woordenlijst*, Leiden, 1923

Kartoatmodjo, M. Soekarto, 'The Discovery of Three New Inscriptions in the District of Klaten (South Central Java)', *Bulletin of the Archaeological Institute of the Republic of Indonesia*, No.8, Djakarta, 1969

Kartohadikoesoemo, Soetardjo, *Desa* (2nd edn), Jogjakarta, 1965

Kats, J., 'Dewi Çri', *TBG*, LVII, afl. 3, 1915, 177-96

Keesing, Felix Maxwell, *The Ethnohistory of Northern Luzon*, Stanford, 1962

Kern, Hendrick, *Rāmāyaṇa Kakawin: Oudjavaansch heldendicht* 's-Gravenhage, 1900

_____, *Verspreide Geschriften*, VI, Pt 6, 249-317, Pt 7, 1-226, Inscripties van den Indischen archipel, 's-Gravenhage, 1917

Korn, Victor Emmanuel, *Het adatrecht van Bali*, S'Gravenhage, 1924

Krom, N.J., 'Epigraphische aantekeningen I II III', *TBG*, LV, afl. 4, 5, 6, 1913, 585-600

_____, (ed), 'Oud-Javaansche oorkonden: Nagelaten transcripties van wijlen Dr J.L.A. Brandes', *VGB*, LX, 1913

_____, 'Epigraphische aantekeningen', *TBG*, LVI, afl. 3 en 4, 1914, 233-56

_____, 'Epigraphische aantekeningen', *TBG*, LVII, afl. 1, 1915, 15-22

_____, 'Epigraphische aantekengingen, Nos XI-XII', *TBG*, LVII afl. 6, 1916, 522-8

_____, 'Epigraphische bijdragen', *BKI*, LXXV, 1919, 8-24

_____, *Inleiding tot de Hindoe-Javaansche Kunst*, vols I-III, 2 herziende druk, 's-Gravenhage, 1923

_____, *Hindoe-Javaansche geschiedenis*, 2 herziende druk, 's-Gravenhage, 1931

Kromodjojo Adi Negoro, raden adipati ario, *Oud-Javaansche Oorkonde op steen uit het afdeeling Modjokerto*, I, 1921?

Kruyt, A.C., 'De rijstmoeder in den Indischen Archipel', *MKAW-L*, XLVII, 1903

_____, 'Gebruiken bij den rijstoogst in enkele streken op Oost-Java', *Mededeelingen van wege het Nederlandsche Zendingsgenootschap*, XLVII, 1903, 125-39

_____, *Het animisme in den Indischen Archipel*, 's-Gravenhage, 1906

Kunthi: Kalawarti basa Djawa, No.3, Th.II, Sapar 1903

Kuntjaraningrat (ed.), *Villages in Indonesia*, New York, 1967

Lambrecht, Francis, *The Mayawyaw Ritual. I. Rice culture and rice ritual*, Publications of the Catholic Anthropological Conference, IV, 1, Washington, 1932, 1-167

Lekkerkerker, C., 'Verbetering en vermeerdering van cultuurgrond op Java', *De Indische Gids*, II, 1, 1929, 521-57

Lekkerkerker, C., *Land en volk van Java*, Groningen-Batavia, 1938

Lekkerkerker, Teunis Cornelis, *Hindoe-Recht in Indonesië*, Amsterdam, 1918

Lerche, Grith and Axel Steensberg, 'Observations on Spade-cultivation in the New Guinea Highlands', *Tools & Tillage*, II, 2, 1973, 87-104

Liefrinck, F.A., 'De Rijstcultuur op Bali', *De Indische Gids*, VIII, 2, 1886 and IX 1, 1887

_____, *Landsverorderingen van Inlandsche Vorsten op Bali*, S'Gravenhage, 1917

_____, *Bali and Lombok: Geschriften*, Amsterdam, 1927

_____, 'Rice Cultivation in Northern Bali', in *Bali: Further Studies in Life, Thought and Ritual*, The Hague, 1969

Leur, J.C. van, *Indonesian Trade and Society: Essays in Asian Social and Economic History* (2nd edn), The Hague, 1967

Lewis, Henry T., *Ilocano Rice Farmers. A comparative study of two Philippine barrios*, Honolulu, 1971

Macdonell, Arthur Anthony, *A practical Sanskrit dictionary, with transliteration, accentuation, and etymological analysis throughout*, reprinted in 1969, London

Maclaine Pont, H., 'Aantekening bij het artikel van Dr van Stein Callenfels: "Bijdragen tot de Topographie van Oost-Java in de Middeleeuwen"', *OV*, 1926, 88-93

_____, 'Eenige oudheidkundige gegevens omtrent de Middeleeuwschen bevloeingstoestand van de zoo-genaamde "woeste gronden van Trik"', *OV*, 1926, 100-29

Majumdar, R.C., *Inscriptions of Kambuja*, Asiatic Society Monograph Series, VIII, Calcutta, 1953

Mallinckrodt, J.,'Grond-en waterrecht in de onder-afdeeling Boetoek', *Het Koloniaal Tijdschrift*, I, 15 Jaargang, 1924

Marriott, McKim (ed), 'Little Communities in an Indigenous Civilization', in *Village India*, Chicago, 1955

Moertono, Soemarsaid, *State and Statecraft in Old Java: a study of the Later Mataram Period, 16th to 19th Century*, Monograph Series, Modern Indonesia Project, Southeast Asia Program, Department of Asian Studies, Cornell University, New York, 1968

Naerssen, F.H. van, 'De Saptopapatti. Naar inleiding van een tekstverbetering in den Nāgarakṛtāgama, *BKI*, XC, 1933, 239-58

_____, 'Twee Koperen Oorkonden van Balitung in het Koloniaal Instituut te Amsterdam Holland', *BKI*, XCV, 1937, 441-61

Naerssen, F.H. van, 'De Brantas en haar waterwerken in den Hindu-Javaanschen tijd', *de Ingenieur*, LIII, 7, 1938

_____, 'Inscripties van het Rijksmuseum voor volkenkunde te Leiden', *BKI*, XCVII, 1938, 501-13

_____, *Oudjavaansche Oorkonden in Duitsche en Deensche Verzamelingen*, Leiden, 1941

_____, 'De Overvaartplaatsen aan de Solo Rivier in de Middeleeuwen', *TAG*, LX, 1943, 622-38, 724-6

_____, 'The Çailendra Interregnum', *India Antiqua, A volume of Oriental Studies*, Leiden, 1947

_____, 'Some Aspects of the Hindu-Javanese Kraton', *Journal of the Oriental Society of Australia*, II, 1, 1963

Naerssen, F.H. van and R.C. de Iongh, *The Economic and Administrative History of Early Indonesia*, Handbuch der Orientalistik, 111 abt.: Indonesian, Malaysia und die Philippinen, Leiden/Köln, 1977

Niel, Robert van, 'Measurement of Change under the Cultivation System in Java, 1837-1851', *Indonesia*, 14, Oct. 1972, 89-109

Nilles, John, 'Digging sticks, spades, hoes, axes and adzes of the Kuman people in the Bismark Mountains in East-Central New Guinea', *Anthropos*, XXXVII-XL, 1942-5, 205-12

Nivideta, *Sister, Kali the Mother* (2nd edn), Calcutta, 1953

Noorduyn, J., 'Further topical notes on the ferry charter of 1358', *BKI*, CXXIV, 1968, 460-80

_____, and H. Th. Verstappen, 'Pūrṇavarman's river-works near Tugu', *BKI*, CXXVIII, 1972, 299-306

Palerm, Angel, 'The agricultural basis of urban civilization in Mesoamerica', in *Irrigation Civilizations: a comparative study. A symposium on method and result in cross-cultural regularities*, Social Science Monographs I, Washington, 1955, 28-41

Pigeaud, Th., *Javaans-Nederlands handwoordenboek*, Groningen, 1938

_____, 'Javanese Gold', *BKI*, CXIV, 1958, 190-6

_____, *Java in the 14th Century: a study in cultural history. The Nāgara-kĕrtāgama by Rakawi Prapañca of Majapahit, 1365, A.D.*, 5 vols (3rd edn), The Hague, 1960-63

Pleyte, C.M., 'Maharaja Cri Jayabhupati, Sunda's oudste bekende vorst. A.D. 1030', *TBG*, LVII, afl. 3, 1915, 200-18

Poerbatjaraka, R. Ng. *Riwajat Indonesia*, Djakarta, 1951

_____, 'De naam Dharmawangça', *TBG*, LXX, 1930, 171-83

Purbo Hadiwidjojo, M.M. and I. Surjo, *Volcanic Activity and its Implications on Surface Drainage: The case of the Kelut volcano, East Java, as an example*. Papers originally presented at the Irrigation Seminar, Malang, 9-23 July 1968

Quaritch Wales, H.G., 'Cosmological Aspect of Indonesian Religion', *Journal of the Royal Asiatic Society of Great Britain and Ireland*, 1959, 100-39

_____, *The Making of Greater India* (2nd edn), London, 1961

Rapporten van de commissie in Nederlandsch-Indie, voor oudheidkundig onderzoek op Java en Madoera, 1905-6. *Oudheidkundige Dienst in Nederlandsch-Indie, Rapporten, 1907*, 86

Redfield, Robert, *The Little community and Peasant society and culture*, Chicago, 1967

Sarkar, H.B., 'Literary and Epigraphic Notes', *Journal of the Greater India Society*, IV, 1, Jan. 1937, 36-42

_____, 'A Geographical Introduction to the Study of Kawi Oorkonden-1', *BKI*, CV, 1949, 107-10

_____, 'Survey of Some Aspects of Old-Javanese Inscriptions of Central Java', in Buddha Prakash (ed.), *Studies in Asian History and Culture*, Meerut, 1970

_____, *Corpus of the Inscriptions of Java* (Corpus Inscriptionum Javanicarum), I and II, Calcutta, 1972

Schrieke, B.J.O., 'Iets over Perdikan-instituut', *TBG*, LVIII, 1919, 391-423

_____, 'Uit de geschiedenis van het adatgrondrecht: De theorie van het zoogenaamde vorstelijk eigendomsrecht', *TBG*, LXI, 1920, 122-90

_____, 'Eenige opmerkingen over ontleening in de Cultuur-ontwikkeling', *Djawa*, VII, afl. 2, 1927, 89-96

_____, *Indonesian Sociological Studies, Pt II, Ruler and Realm*, The Hague, 1957

Selosoemardjan, *Social Changes in Jogjakarta*, New York, 1962

Shetrone, Henry C., 'A unique prehistoric irrigation project', *Annual Report of the Board of Regents of the Smithsonian Institution*, 1945, 379-86

Sircar, D.C., *Indian Epigraphy*, Delhi, 1965

_____, (ed.), *Select Inscriptions bearing on Indian history and civilization*, I, Inscription No.67, Junagarh rock inscription of Rudradaman I, University of Calcutta, 1965, 175-82

Slamet, Ina, *Pokoh-pokoh pembangunan masjaraket desa* (2nd edn), Jakarta, 1965

Slametmuljana, *The Structure of the National Government of Madjapahit*, Djakarta, 1966

Solheim, Wm II, 'An Earlier Agricultural Revolution', *Scientific American*, Apr. 1972, 34-41

Sollewijn Gelpke, J.H.F., 'Het desabestuur op Java. Een bijdrage tot de kennis van Land en Volk', *De Indische Gids*, I, 2, July 1879, 136-44

Stargadt, J., 'Government and Irrigation in Burma: a comparative survey', *Asian Studies*, VI, 1, Apr. 1968, 358-71

———, 'Southern Thai Waterways: Archaeological evidence on agriculture, shipping and trade in the Srivajayan Period', *Man. The Journal of the Royal Anthropological Institute*, New Series, VIII, 1, Mar. 1973, 5-29

Spencer, J.E., 'The Migration of Rice from Mainland Southeast Asia into Indonesia', in Jacques Barrau (ed.), *Plants and the Migrations of Pacific Peoples* (10th Pacific Science Congress), Honolulu, 1963

Stein Callenfels, P.V. van, 'De inscriptie van Kandangan', *TBG*, LVIII, 1919, 359

———, 'Oude oorkonde over Grondenrecht (1025)', *Adatrechtbundel*, 22, Series U, 32, 1923, 413-14

———, 'Bijdrage tot de Topographie van Oost Java in de Middeleeuwen II', *OV*, Bijlage E, 1926, 81-7

———, 'Epigraphica Balica', *VGB*, LXVI, 3, 1925-26

———, 'Bijdragen tot de Topographie van Java in de Middeleeuwen', *Feestbundel*, II, 1927

———, 'De inscriptie van Sukabumi', *MKAW-L*, LXXVIII, 1934, 116-22

———, and L. van Vuuren, 'Bijdrage tot de topografie van de residentie Soerabaja in de 14de eeuw', *TAG*, XLI, Jan. 1924, 67-81

Steinmann, A., 'De op de Boroboedoer afgebeelde planten', *TBG*, LXXIV, 1934, 581-612

Stewart, J.A., 'Kyaukse irrigation, a sidelight on Burmese history', *Journal of the Burma Research Society*, XII, 1921, 1

Stutterheim, W.F., 'Een belangrijke oorkonde uit Kedoe', *TBG*, LXVII, 1927, 172-215

———, 'Oudheidkundige aantekeningen', *BKI*, XC, 1933, 267-99; XCII, 1935, 181-210; XCV, 1937, 397-424

Stutterheim, W.F., 'Iets over raka en rakryan naar aanleiding van Sindok's dynastieke positie', *TBG*, LXXIII, 1933, 159-71

_____, 'Inscriptie op een zuiltje van Papringan', *TBG*, LXXIII, 1933, 96-101

_____, 'Beschreven Lingga van Krapjak', *TBG*, LXXIV, 1934, 85-93

_____, 'Epigraphica', *TBG*, LXXV, 1935, 420-67

_____, 'Het zinrijke van Djalatoenda', *TBG*, LXXVII, 1937, 214-56

_____, and Th. Pigeaud, 'Een Javaansche Oorkonde uit den bloeitijd van Madjapahit', *Djawa*, VI, 1926, 195-204

Suparlan, Parsudi, 'Upatjara Panenan Padi. Sebuah pranata jang telah lenjap dari masjarakat petani[2] di Djawa karena sudah tak berfungsi lagi', *Manusia Indonesia*, Nomor 1-6, tahun ke III, 1969, 49-52

Suzuki, Peter, *The Religious System and Culture of Nias, Indonesia*, S'Gravenhage, 1959

Swellengrebel, J.L., Introduction to *Bali: Life, Thought and Ritual*, The Hague and Bandung, 1960

van der Tuuk, H. Neubronner, *Kawi-Balineesch-Nederlansch woordenboek*, 4 vols, Batavia, 1897-1912

Venkayya, V., 'Irrigation in Southern India in Ancient Times', *Archaeological Survey of India*, Annual Report 1903-04, Calcutta, 1906, 205-11

Verstappen, H. Th., 'Geomorphological observation on Indonesian volcanoes', *Drie Geografische Studies over Java*, Feestbundel ter gelegenheid van het negentigjarig bestaan van het Koninklijke Nederlandsch Aardrijkskundig Genootschap, Leiden, 1963, 237-51

Veth, P.J., *Java*, Geographisch, Ethnologisch, Historisch, I, 2^n druk, Haarlem, 1896-1907

Vogel, J. Ph., 'The Earliest Sanskrit Inscriptions of Java', *Publicaties van den Oudheidkundingen Dienst in Nederlands-Indië*, Deel 1, Batavia, 1925, 15-35

Vollenhoven, C. van, *Het adatrecht van Nederlandsch-Indië*, vols. I-III, (2nd edn), Leiden, 1931

_____, *De Indonesiër en zijn grond*, Leiden, 1932

Veblen, Thorstein Bunde, *The theory of the leisure class: an economic study of institutions*, London

Weatherbee, D., *Aspects of the Ancient Javanese*, Ph.D. Thesis, John Hopkins University, 1968

Wheatley, Paul, 'Agricultural Terracing', *Pacific Viewpoint*, VI, 2 Sept. 1965, 123-44

Williams, *Sir* Monier Monier-, *A Sanskrit-English dictionary: etymologically and philologically arranged with special reference to cognate Indo-European languages* (new edn), E. Leuman, C. Cappeller and others, Oxford, 1951

Winstedt, Richard, *The Malays. A cultural history* (6th edn), London, 1961

Wirjosuparto, Sutjipto, R.M., *Apa sebabnya Kediri dan daerah sekitarnya tampil kemuka dalam sedjarah*, Prasaran untuk Konggres Ilmu Pengetahun Nasional Pertama, Malang, 9 August 1958

Wittfogel, Karl A., *Agriculture: A key to the understanding of Chinese Society past and present*, Canberra, 1970

Wolf, Eric R., *Peasants*, New Jersey, 1966

Wolters, O.W., *Early Indonesian Commerce: a study of the origins of Srivijaya*, New York, 1967

Yamin, Muhammad, *Petulisan Widjaja - Parakrama - Wardana dari Surodaken (Kediri), dengan bertarich Sjaka 1368-T.M. 1447*, Kongress M.I.P.I., Jogyakarta, October 1962

Zoetmulder, P.J., 'The Significance of the Study of Culture and Religion for Indonesian Historiography', in Soedjatmoko (ed.), *An Introduction to Indonesian Historiography*, New York, 1965

GLOSSARY OF INDIGENOUS TERMS USED

ācāryya - priestly scribe
adat - customary law
agem - handful of rice-stalks
air, er, jha - water
ajña - royal word, order
pingsoryajña - ruler's command handed down
ampilan-box containing offerings for the cock-fight
anak - child
anak thāni - farmer
anak wanua - villager
ani-ani - reaping knife used for harvesting rice
anugraha - grant, gift
aripit - small irrigation pipes (Ilocano)
arung - tunnel
aungan - tunnel (Balinese)
pengarung - tunnel builders (Balinese)
terowongan - tunnel (Bah. Indon.)
urung urung - tunnel (New Javanese)
asuji māsa - September, usually time for collecting taxes
atak - land measurement
atap - reeds used for roofing
awig-awig - regulations and laws transmitted orally
awut, uwĕ - grain, possibly rice

badeg - liquor, palm wine
bahu, bau - land measurement of $1^3/4$ acres
bakal, bakalan - to clear virgin land
bañu - water
bañu piṇḍah - flowing water
barih - land measure, size unknown
bekel - official
pembekel - official, usually in charge of taxation
bhādra - September-October
bibit - rice seedlings

bini haji – ruler's wife, usually queens of lesser rank
blah, bĕlah – land measurement
brahman – member of the priestly class in Bali
buat haji – service to the ruler, construction work
buatan wetan – 'made in the east'

cacah – piece of land owned by family
caitra – March-April
śaka – era commencing 78 A.D.
carik – sawah land, dike
caru – rice offerings for chthonic spirits
śrī – illustrious, deity, dewi śrī, rice goddess

dadaptak – reeds
ḍang – honorific, usually for priestly class, i.e. ḍang hyang, ḍang ācāryya
ḍapunta – honorific title
ḍapur – rural community
daun légo légo – offering burnt in the sawah field at harvest time (Sasak)
ḍawuhan – dam, dammed
deśa – district
dĕpa – land measurement of nine square metres
depa agung – land measurement of nine square metres (Balinese)
depa sihwa – probably for smaller fields and garden land
dharma – sacred domain
dharma kamulan – exact meaning not clear
dharmasīma lĕpas – freehold domain
drĕwya – property
drĕwya haji – percentage of produce due to the ruler, ruler's share
ḍukuh – hamlet
dukun – shaman, village priest
ɖusun – village (Sumatra)
dyah – title of prince or princess

gaga – unterraced rice-fields in hills, unirrigated
galagah – a type of reed
galengan – small dikes in sawah (modern term)
gampong – village (Aceh)
gawai – work, also canal or artificial river?

gawai haji - corvee labour
gedong - shed
golongan - group or association of sawah farmers (Bah. Indon.)

haji - chief, ruler
hamat, ha (abbrev.) - certain weight or volume of grain
hulu - head
hulair, huler - head of irrigation works
hulu wras - official in charge of rice supplies
hulu wuatan - supervisor of bridge building?
hyang - supernatural powers, divinity
hyang guru - spiritual master

inan pare - symbolic bridal pair made from rice sheaves (Sasak)

jam-jaman - measuring irrigation water by time
janur - young palm leaves
jawa - grain, possibly rice
jayapattra - record of law case
julung - festival
jung - land measurement of seven acres
juru - official, expert
juru arah - scribe
juru kemong - head of cock-fight arena

kabayan - rural official
kain, ken - length of cloth, wearing apparel
kakawin - Old Javanese poem
kaki - senior member, retired village elder
kalang - certain group of people in Java
kalangan - cock-fight arena
kali - river, canal (kali-canal, Ilocano)
kalima - mentioned with rāmas, (possibly as pangliman, assistant, Bali)
karaeng - similar to rakryān (Macassar)
karya - small land holding, for a single family
kārsa, kā (abbrev.) - a certain weight of gold or silver
kati - a weight of gold or silver
katik - land measure, size unknown
kembang boreh - fragrant ungent
kerta sima - written laws and regulations (Balinese)
kerta sima desa - village regulations
kerta sima subak - subak regulations

kikil - land measurement of $3^1/2$ acres

kilala - a class of people

mangilala drĕwya haji - groups performing special functions for ruler or rakryān

klian - official

klian sĕdahan - official between sedahan agung and sedahan tembuku

klian subak - head of the sekaha subak

kraton - centre of the kingdom, ruler's residence

kudur - priest officiating at ceremonies. Sometimes sang or hyang kudur

makudur - priest

kulina - sawah owner, village 'elite'

kulumpang, watu kulumpang - stone commemorating a land grant

kupang - weight of gold or silver, especially in Majapahit era

kurĕn - spouse, marriage

kurĕnkurĕnan - assembling with wives at a celebration

ladang - slash and burn cultivation

ladu - lava flow

lahar - mud flow (of water and lava material)

lamwit - land measurement

langkat - measurement, span of outstretched thumb and middle finger

lattir - land measurement

legundi - see daun lego lego

lingga - phallic symbol (Śiwa)

anna liṅga - rice cone for offering

lirih - land measurement

lontar - palm

luah prasiddha - sacred river

mahādĕwi - secondary queen

mahārāja - paramount ruler

mancalima - group of eight villages around the centre village

mancapat - group of four villages around the centre village

mantenan - harvest slametan or celebration (Balinese)

temanten pari slametan - rice 'marriage' or harvest celebration (Javanese)

mantra - incantation

mantri, mahāmantri - high court official

mapatih - minister

maren-marenan - means of allocating irrigation water

māsa, mā (abbrev.) - weight (of silver)
mas - gold
mas suwarna - weight (of gold)
mĕgat - high court official, prince
pamĕgat - high court official, prince
samĕgat - high court official, prince
samgat - high court official, prince
metik - 'to pluck'
slamĕtan metik - harvest or 'first fruits' ritual
tukang metik - one who divines an auspicious day to begin harvesting
mpunta - honorific title
mula - when used in connection with dawuhan meaning obscure
(mula - root)
muwah - in addition to

nāgara - the town
nāgara agung - land outside the city limits, held by princes
manca nāgara - outer limits of kingdom
negorij - village (Minihasa)
nāyaka - official employed by rakryāns
nāyaka air - irrigation official
nini - rice 'mother'
nini pantun - see inan paré (Balinese)

pacĕrakan - land measurement, nine square metres
pacul - (stone) hoe used for sawah farming
padas - compact volcanic material
padi - rice in the field
pakārungan - part of cock-fight arena
pangkur - rural court official
pangulu bañu, pengulu bañu - irrigation official
parameçwari - title of the chief queen
paron, maron - dividing the products of the soil (share-cropping)
pasayak - association of sawah farmers (Ilocano)
pati (h) - official, steward, usually connected with the court
pati tambak - steward of royal fisheries
paruwus - assistant to court official
parujar - assistant, or representative of court official
pekasih - subak members who perform maintenance duties

pemangku - subak priest
pemarik - see pipil
pendedeng - 'drying out' period after childbirth
pencar - rice sheaf
perdikan desa - freehold district
perdikan darma - freehold religious domain
pesemaian - rice seedbed
phalguna - month of February-March
picul - a certain weight, to carry
pipil - record of sawah farmers' names etc. on lontar leaves
pirak - silver
pisis - monetary value in fifteenth century
praśasti - edict
pūja - annual rural community celebration
pamūja - contributions to the festival of puja
punggawa - district head (sedahan agung in Bali)
punah - see muwah
punta - see mpu

ragi yu (ga) - patterned cloth
raka, rakai, ratu - chief, ruler of principality
rakryān, rakaryān - chief, prince
rāma - village head, elder
rāma deśa - district head or leader
rāma marata - apparently retired rāma
rāma tpi sering - rāmas of neighbouring villages
rāma tuha - probably as rāma maratā
karamān - council of elders, sometimes used for district under a rāma
rawa - marshland, morass
rĕnĕk - marshland

sabit - sickle
saji - offerings
saluran - see wĕluran
sambandha - reason, purpose
sang - honorific
sapasuk - entire surrounding agricultural land
sātak - a measurement

sawah – wet-rice fields
sawah tadahan – terraced fields dependant on rainwater
sawah sorotan – terrace irrigation by pipes
pasawahan – terraced fields
sawi – demarcation line or cord
sawung – fighting cock
saya – assistant to subak official
sayugan – flume (Ilocano)
sedahan – agricultural official
sedahan agung – court or government official, district head
sedahan jeh – modern sedahan tembuku
sedahan tembuku – subordinate to sedahan agung
sega polong – rice-ball
sekaha – association
sekaha subak – irrigation association
sekaha subak tlabah – association of sekaha subaks
selokan – ditch, channel (Malay)
semangat – life force, spirit
sirih, sereh – betel, areca
siku – Balinese measurement
sīma – grant, usually of land, freehold land or domain
slametan – communal feast
slametan sedaka bumi – feast to celebrate harvest
slametan metik – 'first fruits' celebration before commencing harvest
subak – irrigation association (modern Balinese)
subaki – appears to be a place-name (OJO XCIV-V)
sudra – lowest caste (in Bali)
susuk, manusuk – to celebrate a freehold from virgin land
sus(k) kulumpang – foundation stone
suwak – probably earthern walls around sawah fields
kesuwakan – irrigation association (modern – subak)

tahil – measure of gold or silver, later applied to tax
talang – aqueduct, usually of bamboo
tameng – dike, dam
tamya – tameng
tambak, tamwak – dam, pond, lake
tamwaka – to build a dam

matamwak - official probably in charge of irrigation installations
tambuku - distribution block (tembuku, temuku - Balinese)
tampah - area measurement particularly for sawah fields
tampah haji - royal land measurement
tangan - measurement
tanggul - dam wall, barrage
thāni, tāni - farmland, rarely applied to farmers
tawan - court official, see pangkur and tirip
tĕgal, tĕgalan - dry-rice land, open plain, unterraced
tka (tĕka) dlaha ning dlaha - to the end of time
tĕnah - land measurement, water measurement by volume
tĕnah winih - estimated amount of seed grain
tpi (tĕpi) siring - neighbouring villages
terowongan - tunnel (Bah. Indon.)
tetajen - cock-fight (Balinese)
sima tĕtajen - regulations for cock-fight
tetajen desa - cock-fight at village level
tetajen lewih - cock-fight arranged by the kraton
tĕtajen subak - sekaha subak cock-fight
tiga sana - tax on rice fields
tinulad - copied
tirip - official, see pangkur and tawan
tirtha - sacred bathing-place
tlabah - see wĕluran
turun turun - tithe, tax levied on bundle of rice
tuha, tua, tuwa - elder
tuha kalang - elder of the group of kalangs
tuha wanua - headman of village
matuha, rāma matuha - elder

umah - probably farmhouse, communal house
undagi, undahagi - skilled worker, craftsman, excluding metal
                                              worker (pande)
undagi pangarung - tunnel builder (Old Balinese)
ulu-ulu - present-day group connected with irrigation. See
                         golongan, perhaps formerly wulu wulu
upapatti - court priests, assessors
uluran - area supplied with irrigation water from same source.
                         See wĕluran

wadihati - assistant at ceremony

waduk - reservoir, basin (Bah. Indon.)
wadwa - official, servant
wahuta - sometimes sang wahuta - priestly official at ceremonies
wanua, wanwa - village
wariga - rural astrologer
watĕk, watak - district under ruler's jurisdiction
water - 'fence' (not occurring before fourteenth century)
wayang - puppet performance
wĕdihan - ceremonial cloth for men's wear
wĕdihan yu - pair or set of cloth, kain and turban
wĕluran - channel, conduit
winkas, winĕkas - representative at ceremonial function
winih - rice seedgrain
pawinih - seedbed
suwinih - water tax (Balinese)
wha - unit of weight (of rice yield)
wras, bĕras - husked rice
wuatan, wwatan - reservoir, large dam, bridge

yawa, yawae (Dyak) *yaba urĕ* (Batak) - grain, possibly rice
yoni - female symbolic counterpart of lingga
yuga - ceremonial cloth consisting of two pieces

INDEX OF INSCRIPTIONS

Tugu c.450 A.D.	xvii, 6,n.20, 22
Canggal 732 A.D.	xiv, 4
Plumpungan 752 A.D.	xiv, 35, 117
Dinaya 760 A.D.	xiv, 9, 115, 117
Kalasan 778 A.D.	90, 123
Kĕlurak 782 A.D.	123
Hariñjing 804 A.D.	xiv, xviii, 8, 20, 23, 29, 62, 134, 135
Dieng 809 A.D.	35, 36, 79, n.7, 86
Kamalagi 821 A.D.	65
Karangtĕngah 824 A.D.	xiv, 34, 40, 120
Kuṭi 840 A.D.	xvii, 115, 123
Tri Tĕpusan 840 A.D.	59
Śrī Kahulunan 842 A.D.	40, 86, 92, 123
Perot 850 A.D.	60, 90n. 34
Siwagĕrha 856 A.D.	xiv, 27
Kañcana 860 A.D.	85, 113, 114
Wukiran (Pereng) 862 A.D.	xiv, 120
Wanua Tĕngah 863 A.D.	38
Śri Manggala II 874 A.D.	37
Bintang Mas A 878 A.D.	114
Ngabean I & II 879 A.D.	33, 34, 38, 83, 117, 121
Mamali (Polengan V)	69
Wuatan Tija 880 A.D.	124
Ngabean V 881 A.D.	117
Papringin 882 A.D.	63
Balingawan 891 A.D.	114, 126
Bĕbĕtin A (Bali) 896 A.D.	29
Taji 901 A.D.	94, 96, 112, 113, 115, 121, 123
Panggumulan (Kembang Arum) 902 A.D.	70-71, 96, 120-121
Rubukubu 905 A.D.	114
Palĕpangan 906 A.D.	35, 36, 37, and n.102, 63, 114
Mantyāsih I 907 A.D.	117-118, 123, 127
Sangsang (Amsterdam) 907 A.D.	89, 95, 122

Jayapattra, unknown origin 907 A.D.	95
Sugih Manik 915 A.D.	124
Lintakan 919 A.D.	69, 115
Hariñjing B 921 A.D.	20, 23, 116
Charter, unknown origin 924 A.D.	88
Hariñjing C 926 A.D.	as for Hariñjing B
Kinawĕ 927 A.D.	94
Sangguran (Minto) 928 A.D.	115, 120, 124
Sarangan 929 A.D.	9, 134
Bakalan 934 A.D.	xviii, 9, 23, 29, 51-52, 89, 134, 137
Mahārāja Nāri 1015 A.D.	93
Batuan (Bali) 1022 A.D.	30
Klungkung (Bali) 1022 A.D.	28, 42
Sang Hyang Tapak (Sunda) 1030 A.D.	52
Kĕlagyan 1037 A.D.	xviii, 4, 13, 18, 23, 33, 34, 78, 86, 113, 127, 135, 147
Pucangan (Calcutta Stone) 1041 A.D.	xiv, 13
Sarwadharma 1268 A.D.	64, 72, 114
Jaya Song jayapattra 1350 A.D.	67
Kandangan 1350 A.D.	xviii, 20, 23, 134
Trawulan 1358 A.D.	17 n.46
Karang Bogĕm 1387 A.D.	26, 39, 61, 93
Biluluk II 1391 A.D.	58
Suradakan 1447 A.D.	17, 38, 85, 134
Trailokyapuri 1486 A.D.	xix, 23, 29, 42, 64, 65, 134

GENERAL INDEX

Adams, R., 6-7, 75, 133

Adat, law, x, 54, 55, 66, 76, n.3, 97
Balinese lawbooks, viii, x; lawsuit of 907 A.D., 95; of 1350 A.D., 67f;
legal documents, *jayapattra* xviii, 67, 95; *kerta sima*, viii, 44; *kerta sima subak*, viii, ix, 44, 45, 48, 50, 51;
inscriptions as, xix,
transmitted orally (*awig-awig*) 44

Agastya, sage, 115, 117

Agrarian administration, ix, x,
administrative provinces (*watěks*) 84, 86,
centralized (court), 7, 53, 75, 89, 97,
Indianized form of, 97,
Sekaha subak, 43,
village, x, 7, 54, 55, 56,
in outer provinces, 84, 86

Agricultural land, 33, 54, 65, 69, 96, 117,
see also, *Sawah* land

Airlangga, East Javanese ruler, viii, 4, n.15, 18, 23, 34, 42, 78, 82, 86, 93, 116, 135

Akkeren, P. van, 59, 101, 102

Alisjahbana, S.T., 91

Ancestors, 56, 67, 123, 125, 131

Ancient Java, vii, 3-4, 6, 7-8, 14, 16, 20, 21, 25, 30, 36, 40, 42, 53, 55, 74, 81, 82, 88, 89, 92, 95, 96, 112, 113, 122, 135

Anjasmoro Ranges, 9, 13, 19, 24, 130, maps 1 and 2

Arjuna Volcano, 12f.

Areca plantations (*sirih*), 117

Artificial lakes, 21, 27, 61

Bali, vii, 15, n.40 and 41, 31, 40, 41, 49, 65, 67, 81, 82, 83, 103, 111, 127, 134

Balinese,
adat, viii, x, 44-5;
agricultural festivals, 113;
irrigation guilds, 41-42;
land and water measurements, 39, 40;
ritual sacrifice, 116;
social system, 58

Balitung, Javanese ruler, 8, 89, 117, 131

Bamboo, 7, 25, 26, 29, 36, 107, 110f

Bangsri, 19, map 2

Bhagawanta Bari, builders of Hariñjing project, xx, 62, 135.

Birkelbach, A., 42, n.121, 45f

Bosch, F.D.K., xiii, 71

Brandes, J.L.A., xii, xv, 134

Brangkal River, 19, 134, map 1

Brantas River, 2, 9, 10, 12, 17-20, 78

Bridges (causeways), 5, 8, 22, 26, 74

Briti, 135, map 2

Buchari, M., xi, xiii, 13, n.38, 126

Burma, irrigation works, 21, 23, 24

Cambodia (Angkor), 2, 21, 23

Canals, xvii, 3, 8, 21, 24, 29, 62, 74, 116

Casparis, J.G. de, xii, xiv, n.18, 27-28, 59, 62, 63, 65, 131

Central Java, 9, 74, 92, 117, 126, 130, 131, 133, 134

Ceremonial, xviii, 34, 57, 113, 114, 115, 116, 121, 123, 128, 129

Ceremonies,
canal, 116;
consecration, xx, 118, 119, 121, 122;
foundation, xvii, 34, 57, 115, 116, 123;
land grant, 116-26;
rice-growing, 104-105;
rice harvest, 104, n.12, 105-11

Ceylon (Sri Lanka), 1, 21

Charters, *see* Inscriptions

Chinese sources, 82, 92

Cohen Stuart, A.B., xii, 115

Collier, D., 7, 75, 133

Conduits (*wĕluren*), 9, 20, 21, 29, 31, 42, 50

Council of elders (*tuha wanua*) 7, 53, 55, 74, 84

Curse formula in agrarian ceremonies, 121, 123-25

Damais, L.C., xii, xiii

Dams (*dawuhan*), 8, 20, 22-25, 26, 27, 49, 74;
built by Airlangga, 18f., 23, 86, 116; by Rakryān Mangibil, 26, 28, 52, 116;
dam construction, 7, 9, 20, 23, 49-50, 61;
diversion dam, 21, 22;
restoration of, 20, 23, 134

Dieties, *see* Gods

Dike (*tambak*), 22, 26-28, 42, 46, 50, 124

Distribution block (*tambuku*), 31, 32, 50

Dry-field rice cultivation (*tĕgal*) 1-2, 5, 16, 33, 117

Durga (goddess), connection with rice, 103, 112

Duyvandak, P. Th., 116, n.42

Earth Mother, 103, 104, 112

East Java, 2, 8, 9, 17, 51, 61, 74, 107, 117, 130, 133, 134

Eck, R. van, 128, 129, 130

Eck, R. van and F.H. Liefrinck, viii, 44, 49

Edicts, *see* Inscriptions

Eerde, J.C. van, 104, 105, 106, 111

Farmers (*anak thāni*), vii, viii, xiii, xxi, 18, 21, 22, 25, 32, 35, 43, 51, 55, 56, 73

Festivals of the agricultural year, 112-16, 118, 127

Filipino terrace cultivation, 4, 5, n.17

Fisher, C.A., 1, 3

Floods, effect on *sawah* cultivation, 18, 21, 22, 26, 27

Flumes, 5, 21

Foundation stone (*kulumpang*), 115, 121, 122-23, 125f; *watu sima*, 126

Freehold grants (*sīma*)
agricultural land (*perdikan-darma*), xviii, xix, 69, 85, 90, 94, 132;
dams, 23, 86;
districts (*desa perdikan*), 117;
estates, 69, 84;
garden land, 65, 69;
sawah land, 35, 37, 40, 65, 85, 92-3.

Fukeo Ueno, 72, n.45

Gedang, 19, map 2

Geertz, C., 109, 110, 111

Gio-Linh (Vietnam),
 terrace complex, 5, 130

Gods worshipped in agrarian
 society, 102, 103, 104, 113, 114,
 116, 119, 120, 121, 122, 123,
 125

Gonggrijp, G., 82

Goris, R., xii, xvi, 31, 65, 118

Gorkom, K.W., 31f

Grader, C.J., 102, 110-111

Groslier, B.P., 2

Guilds connected with *sawah*
 cultivation, viii, xvi, xviii,
 38, 41-51, 69, 117, 118, 135

Haar, B. ter, x

Hariñjing dam and conduit, xx, 8f.,
 20, 23, n.56, 62, 134, 135

Hariñjing River, 8-9, 20, map 2

Hayam Wuruk, ruler of Majapahit,
 10, 11, 93

Hinloopen Labberton, D. van, 11

Ho, Robert, 16

Ilocano, 29, 41

India, Indian, xv, 1, 2, 3, 4, 6,
 8, 9, 53, 66, 74, 75, 76, 77, 96,
 97, 102, 103, 104

Indo-China, 2, 4

Indo-Javanese Period, xi,
 xiv, 6, 10, 13, 17, 21, 42, 54,
 66, 97, 117, 133, 135

Indonesia, Indonesian, viii, ix, xv,
 2, 6, 16, 41, 53, 54, 91, 96, 99,
 100, 104, 120, 125

Irrigation Associations (*sekaha
 subaks*), viiif., 28, 41-51, 134,
 135

Irrigation channels, 5, 21, 22, 25,
 28, 29, 31, 33, 51, 52, 73, 102,
 104, 131

Irrigation management, viii, ix, 2,
 3, 8, 49, 53, 58, 59, 134, 135

Irrigation pipes (*talang*), 26, 27,
 29, 33, 51, 66, 73, 104

Irrigation principles, 21, 22-52
 techniques, 2, 8, 58, 74;
 terminology, 22, 23, 26-32

Irrigation projects,
 inscriptions concerning, xiv, xvii-
 xviii, xx;
 large-scale, 8, 9, 21, 22, 74, 80
 97, 135;
 in other lands, 21;
 privately-owned, xx, 134;
 small-scale, 7, 8, 22, 25-26, 74

Jay, Robert, 32

Jeruk Legi, 19, map 2

Juynboll, H.H., 26

Kali Konto, 9, 20, map 2

Kali Porong, 18, 19, map 2

Kandangan dam, 20, 134, map 2

Kañjuruhan, East Javanese kingdom,
 xiv, 74

Karangkates dam, 135, map 2

Karangrejo, 18, map 2

Kartahadikoesomo, Soetardjo, 58

Kediri, 2, 9, 12, 18, 20 (Daha),
 93, map 2

Kelagen, 19, map 2

Kělagyan dam, 18f., 23, 86, 116, 135

Kelud volcano, 9-12, 13, n.38, 14, 16, 17, 19 and n.48, 132, map 2

Kemiri, 18, map 2

Kěrtanagara, ruler of Singasari, 64, 114

Kertosono, 18, map 2

Kingship, 8, 74, 75, 77-78, see also *Mahārāja*

Korn, V.C., 41, 52, n.133

Kraton, see *Sawah* cultivation under

Krom, N.J., xiii, 103, 130

Kromodjojo Adi Negoro, R.A.A., xviii, 28

Kromong River, 9, 12, 13, 20, 31, map 1

Kruyt, A.C., 107-8, 111

Ladang (swidden), 3, 33

Land ownership, 56-7, 66-8, transfer of, xix, 39f., 117-18

Land rights, ix, 66-68, 81, 86

Landean River, 9, 12, 20, map 1

Lava (*ladu*), 14, 15

Law, Indonesian customary, see, *Adat*

Lekkerkerker, C., 1-2, 3, 32

Lekkerkerker, T.C., 66, 82

Leur, J.C. van, 6

Lewis, H.T., 41

Liefrinck, F.A., ix, 37, 83, 110, 127

Lingga, 125, 126

Lokapala, Javanese ruler, 84, 85

Lombok, 104, 112

Lontar leaves, ix, xviii, 35, 121

Maclaine Pont, H., xix, 11, n.32, 23, 24, 30, 31

Madagascar, viii, 1, 41

Mahārāja, Sovereign Ruler, *sawah* cultivation under the, 74-98
women ranking as, 91, 93

Majapahit,
era, xvi, 42, 66, 83f., 89, 113, 123, n.64, 127, 135;
kingdom, viii, 8, 9, 11, n.32, 13, and n.38, 132, 134;
kings, 82, 128

Measurements used in *sawah* cultivation,
for irrigation water, 31-32, 40;
for *sawah* fields, xviii, 35-41

Menhir, 5, 125, 126

Moertono, S., 100-101

Mojokerto, 18, 19

Naerssen, F.H. van, xiii, 10, 17, n.45, 53, 63, 64, 93, 97

Nāgarakěrtāgama, ix, xiii, 10, 13, n.37, 81, 112

Netherlands Colonial Government, viif, x, 59, 65

New Guinea,
farming implements, 3 and n.14

Northern Luzon, viii, 1, 41

Officials, agrarian,
court, xv, xvi, 7, 60, 85, 87-90f.,
irrigation, 45-46, 61-65
village, xv, 7, 60-61, 120

Old Balinese inscriptions, xi, xii, xv, xvi, 26, 28, 29-30, 31, 65, 118-19

Old Javanese inscriptions, xi-xix, 13, 61, 91, 92-94, 95, 117-19, 120, 133, 134

Old Javanese (*kawi*), viii, xi, xvii, 29, 31, 65, 111, 119, 120, 128

Pamotan, 19, map 2

Pararaton, 10, 11, 13, n.37, 19

Parsudi Suparlan, 104, n.12

Penanggungan Mountain, 12, 29, 31, 131, map 1

Pigeaud, Th., xiii, 3, 11 and n.32, 36, n.99, 58, 60, 64, 66, 68, 72, 89

Pikatan River, 9, 12, 13, 19, 20, 28, 31, 130, map 1

Place-names, connected with *sawah* cultivation, xv, xviii, 27, 29, 54, 133, 134

Poerbatjaraka, R. Ng., xiii

Ponds, 26, 28

Priests, 6, 46, 76, 85, 107-8, 122, 123, 124

Princes (*rakryāns*), 36, 76, 84, 86, 87-9, 91, 94
Princess of Lasĕm, East Java, 61, 93,

Purbo Hadiwidjojo, M.M., and I. Surjo, 10, n.30, 16

Queens in Javanese agrarian society, 86, 91, 92, 93, 94

Quaritch Wales, H.G., 102

Rainfall, rain water, 15, 16, 21, 26, 28, 33

Rakryān Mangibil, Sindok's consort, 9, 26, 28, 52, n.133, 89, 116, 135

Rama, ideal king, 77, 78, 98

Rāmāyaṇa, 27f., 78, 80, 98, 121, 122

Religious aspects of agrarian life in Java, 6, 43, 54, 76, 77, 99-100, 101, 107, 108, 126, 127, 128
see also religious domains and temples

Religious domains (*dharmasīma lĕpas*), ix, 38, 69, 71, 84, 85, 95

Reservoir (*wuatan, dawuhan*), 5, 8, 21, 22, 23, 26

Retaining walls (*wuatan*), 21, 26

Rice goddess (Śri), 102-104, 105, 106, 107, 108, 109

Rice harvest, 82, 105-106, 107, 108, 110, 113

Rice Mother (*nini*), 108, 110, 111

Rice rituals, xvii, 99, 101, 104, 105-106, 110-11, 122

Ritual cock-fighting, 112, description of, 128-130; religious significance of, 127, 128, 130; *subak*, 45, 129

Rivers (*kali*) connection with *sawah* cultivation, xvii, 9, 10, 12, 17-20, 21, 131-32

Ruler (*raka*), 36, 49, 53, 74-6, 77, 79-82, 87-8, 91, 94, 98

Rules and regulations, *kerta sima*, viii, ix, 44, 46f., 48, 49-50, 51, 52, 72

Śailendra, Central Javanese dynasty, 8, 74, 92

Sanctuaries connected with *sawah* cultivation, xi, 37, 80, 83f., 93, 115, 117, 120, 130-32

Sanskrit, xi, xiv, 4, 76, 120

Sarkar, H.B., xii, xv, xvi, 35,
  n.98, 37, 63, n.22, 70, 90,
  n.36, 94, n.48, 115, 117, 119,
  120, 122, 123, 124, 125, 127

Sasak rice ritual, 104, 106

Sawah cultivation in Ancient Java,
  antiquity of, 1, 9, 12, 30;
  continuity of, 1, 134;
  development, 17, 74, 133, 134;
  earliest centres, viii, 6, 7,
    8-9, 10, 12;
  hazards, 9-20;
  long history of, 2, 135;
  methods of, 32-34, 55

Sawah cultivation under *kraton*
  supervision, 74-98;
  bond between court and village,
    97-98;
  centralised authority, 7, 53,
    75, 89, 96-97;
  officials, xix, 7, 35, 45f., 76,
    87, 90f.;
  structure of Indo-Javanese
    kingdom, 84-86;
  supervision by *raka, see* ruler

Sawah cultivation at village level,
  53-73, 97;
  autonomous settlements, 54-55;
  communal nature of village,
    55, 133
  connection with neighbouring
    villages (*tpi sering*),
    xviii, xx, 35, 54, 55, 96f.
  dual role of village, 96;
  village administration, *see*
    villages;
  village-court interdependence,
    96-98

Sawah land,
  communal land, 55, 72, 116f.;
  deed of sale of, 40, 69-70;
  establishing new *sawahs*, 44, 54,
    55, 66-7,117;
  mortgaging, 64, 70-1, 77-8, 80,
    93, 126;
  purchasing, 68-9;
  surveying, viii, 35-41, 102

Schrieke, B.J.O., 2

Sedana (Sadana) Śri's consort,
  102, 108

Segodang, 19, map 2

Sekaha subak, see Irrigation
  Associations

Selorejo dam, 20, n.53, map 2

Selosoemardjan, 118, n.47

Serbo, 18, 19, map 2

Sindok, East Javanese ruler, xix,
  9, 33, 89, 93, 131, 134, 135

Slawe, dam, 31, 135, map 1

Sollewijn Gelpke, J.H.F., 35, n.98,
  100,

Solo River, 17, n.45, 46, 131

Source material, ix-xix

Southeast Asia, 1, 21

Spencer, J.E., 1

Spirits, 99, 100, 122
  of ancestors, 123, 125, 126

Śri, *see* rice goddess

Śri Kahulunan, Central Javanese
  queen, 86, 92, 123

Srinjing conduit, 20, 29, map 2

Stein Callenfels, P.V. van, xii, 9,
  19, 29, 42

Stutterheim, W.F., xii, 63, 87, 131

Sumatra, xi, 1, 14

Swellengrebel, J.L., 29, 30

Tameng, 28, map 1

Tanks, 5, 8, 26

Taxes,
  exemption from xi, 83, 85f.;
  on irrigation water, 49, 50, 81;

Taxes,
  land, vii, xi, xv, 39;
  rice, (*tiga sana*), 37, n.102, 82, 83;
  rice yield as basis for, 8, 39;
  royal revenue, 22, 113, 127, 138;
  tax collectors, 88, 90

Temples connected with *sawah* cultivation, 6, 12, 13, 78, 80, 127, 128, 130-32;
  commemorating irrigation projects, 132;
  for defense purposes, 24f., 30f.;
  funerary, 37, 92;
  upkeep of, 37, 117, 132

Terrace cultivators, 4-5

Terracing, 4, 5, 21, 28, 33, 93, 130-31;
  in Gio-Linh (Vietnam), 5, 130

Tools for *sawah* cultivation, 3, 34

Trung, 19, map 2

Tulangan, 19, map 2

Tulodong, ruler, 20, 69, 115

Tunnels, irrigation, viii, 22, 29-31, 74

Veth, P.J., 4

Village head, *rama*, 7, 52, 53, 55, 58, 59-60, 61, 68, 69, 71, 74, 92, 97

Villages, 53-55
  administered by, 7, 53, 55, 84;
  bureaucracy, 60-65;
  organization, 56-59, 66;
  cosmic classification, 58-59

Volcanoes,
  effect on *sawah* cultivation, 9-11, 12-16

Vollenhoven, C. van, vii, x, 54, 56, 66, 73

Waringin Anom, 18

Waringin Pitu (sapta), 18, 85, map 2

Water, irrigation,
  distribution, xviii, 29, 31, 32, 43, 47, 49-50, 72;
  payment for, xviii, 64, 72, 81
  place-names connected with, 27, 134;
  tax (*suwinih*), 49, 50, 83

Water rights, ix, 49, 72-73, 81, 82

Wayang, 121, 122

Welirang Mountain, 12, 13, 19, 130, map 1

Wet-rice cultivation, *see sawah* cultivation

Wheatley, P., 4-5, 125, 130

Winstedt, R., 99f.

Wirjosuparto Sutjipto,R.M., xviii, 2, 3, 17, n.45, 26, 52, n.133, 103, n.9

Wolters, O.W., 8

Women in agrarian society, 91-96;
  holding high rank, 89, 91;
  as land owners, 93-4;
  in legal affairs, 95;
  taking part in land grant ceremonies, 95-6, 121, 122;
  in rice harvest, 106, 107, 110

Yamin, M., 85

Zoetmulder, P.J., 99